CROSSCURRENTS *Modern Critiques*

CROSSCURRENTS *Modern Critiques*
Harry T. Moore, *General Editor*

*Warren French*

# The Social Novel

## AT THE END OF AN ERA

WITH A PREFACE BY

*Harry T. Moore*

Carbondale and Edwardsville

SOUTHERN ILLINOIS UNIVERSITY PRESS

FEFFER & SIMONS, INC.

London and Amsterdam

*For my Mother,*
*Mrs. Helen W. French*

FIRST PUBLISHED, FEBRUARY 1966
SECOND PRINTING, MAY 1967

WARREN FRENCH, who teaches at the University of Missouri at Kansas City, has written books on Frank Norris, John Steinbeck, and J. D. Salinger and has edited A Companion to "The Grapes of Wrath," a valuable and well-documented study of the Dust Bowl, the "Okies," and other phenomena of the thirities. Now, in The Social Novel at the End of an Era, he revisits that troubled decade, looking at the work of several novelists.

He offers some surprises. He does not, for example, deal with any of the group of writers of the so-called proletarian school, and he does not (except in passing) take up the work of one of the notable social novelists of the period, James T. Farrell, who wrote of the Irish middle class in Chicago. Rather unexpectedly, Mr. French examines a book by William Faulkner and one by Ernest Hemingway. John Steinbeck would of course be anticipated, and Mr. French gives us a fresh view of The Grapes of Wrath (In Dubious Battle, Steinbeck's other outstanding social novel, receives only incidental mention). Mr. French also grants consideration to the pair of novels, now little known, which in 1939 shared the American Booksellers' Award with The Grapes of Wrath: Dalton Trumbo's Johnny Got His Gun and Elgin Groseclose's Ararat. There is also a discussion of Robert Penn Warren's Night Rider (1938), a story of the Kentucky "tobacco wars" of the early twentieth century.

Much of this, then, is new ground, terrain not covered in other studies of the social novel. Mr. French begins with a useful survey of the end of the era—between-wars period—mentioned in the title of this book. It was at the close of this period that Faulkner, Hemingway, and Steinbeck brought out the novels Mr. French explores in the main part of his study: The Hamlet, For Whom the Bell Tolls, and The Grapes of Wrath. He provides a thorough background for the study of each of them.

Faulkner is much else, but he is a social novelist, especially in The Hamlet. Mr. French, who from 1948 to 1950 taught at the University of Mississippi, is well acquainted with Faulkner's state and home town. In providing background material for The Hamlet, Mr. French looks at the careers of Senators Vardaman and Bilbo and of Congressman Rankin—relevantly, as the reader will see, for after consulting this expertly documented account, he will have a much fuller acquaintance than before with the Snopeses and their contemporaries. When Mr. French comes to The Grapes of Wrath, he not only analyses the social forces that motivate the story, but he also presents a most interesting discussion of the historical agrarian idealism which underlies it. In the case of For Whom the Bell Tolls, he shifts his focus from the purely American scene to take up the prophetically viewed troubles of an American in "A Troubled World."

This is a distinctly individualized book; I don't know any other that is quite like it. As I said earlier, it covers new terrain. I think that all students and readers of the modern novel, and of the modern American novel in particular, will find this study stimulating.

Now and then I differ with Mr. French, as almost everyone disagrees with parts of any book of this kind; I have elsewhere expressed myself about what I consider some of the limitations of The Grapes of Wrath and For Whom the Bell Tolls. Mr. French says the reason for my attitude is that I am interested primarily in "artistic" novels. That may well be, but I certainly served an apprenticeship to the social novel, and was writing publicly about Steinbeck when Mr. French was in high school. Today I read social novels as eagerly as any other kind—when they are good. Proust certainly wrote a social novel, and that is what the Russians (some of whom are pretty good) turn out regularly. Some of the newer German work—of Heinrich Böll, Günter Grass, and Uwe Johnson—is social as well as symbolical. There is nothing wrong with the genre itself, which can be fairly inclusive, as Mr. French shows. In reading what he says about Hemingway's Spanish-war novel, my respect for that book has increased somewhat. Nothing is likely to make me care very much for The Grapes of Wrath, which seems to me full of sentimentality and quackery, however much the author "means well." But even those who don't care for that book must admit that it is a milestone in the history of the American social novel; and we inevitably teach it in our courses. Mr. French's projection of the background of this novel, as of the others he discusses here, remains highly valuable.

I for one am extremely glad that he wrote this book, and I hope that other readers will feel likewise.

HARRY T. MOORE

Southern Illinois University
September 6, 1965

# ACKNOWLEDGMENTS

MUCH OF Chapter Two has appeared in altered form in the Fall, 1964, issue of the *Midcontinent American Studies Journal,* under the title "The Background of Snopesism in Mississippi Politics."

This book grows out of a seminar in American fiction during the 1930's that I conducted at Kansas State University in the fall of 1963. I am grateful to the dozen graduate students whose questions directed my research, and most especially to Mrs. Laura Greene, who remained interested enough in the project to read the completed manuscript.

After Professor Harry Moore suggested that I write this book, a generous research grant from the College of Arts and Sciences of Kansas State University made it possible for me to spend the summer of 1964 in Madison, Wisconsin, collecting materials and organizing the presentation. I particularly wish to thank the libraries of the University of Wisconsin and the Wisconsin State Historical Society for granting me the use of their facilities.

W. F.

CONTENTS

# The Social Novel

## AT THE END OF AN ERA

# *1* THE END OF AN ERA

A LONG-SICK WORLD died a protracted and agonizing death between March 15, 1939, and June 15, 1940. These dates are not arbitrary. On March 15, 1939, troops of Nazi Germany, Hungary, and Romania occupied what the Munich arrangements had left of independent Czechoslovakia, thus irrevocably destroying British Prime Minister Neville Chamberlain's wistful hope that Hitler's ambitions could be contained by appeasement and that there might be "peace in our time." Fifteen months later, on June 15, 1940, Paris fell to Hitler's mechanized hordes.

The actual declaration of war on September 3, 1939, following German moves against Poland, was but one of a series of incidents that the rape of Czechoslovakia had made inevitable. Not until the fall of Paris, nine and a half months later, was it driven home to a world whose sickness had been evasion and self-delusion that its end had come. It would be hard to overemphasize both the actual and symbolic significance of the German occupation of Paris, for the "city of light" had been the fashionable and cultural capital not just of France but of the whole now prostrate democratic world. The city's significance was caught best, not in pompous political pronouncements that followed the French collapse, but in the sentimental lyrics of Jerome Kern and Oscar Hammerstein II's popular song, "The Last Time I Saw Paris." Borrowing their title for a book of reminiscences whose uncommon popularity showed how the fall of Paris had moved even the remote American public, Elliott Paul, one of the most diehard expatriates, summed up in his last chapter the meaning of a fateful day.

> In future years will always be remembered the day of the black rain, when all those who could or would had fled, and the others were waiting. Some said it was because of oil from blown-up tanks and others believed it might be a deadly gas sent by the Germans. A few thought and tens of thousands hoped it was the end of the world.
>
> It was the end of a world in which Paris was supreme, in which France was alive, in which there was a breath of freedom. There was oil in the blackened air, and soot in the rain, and the wretched city was pressed upon by the lowering sky. Greasy buildings, empty. Dingy pavements, bare.[1]

When had this era that ended in the black rain begun? We have become accustomed to regarding the two dizzying decades of boom-and-bust between two world wars as a unique entity. As passing years, however, give us greater perspective on the history of our own time, we begin to recognize that the years between 1919 and 1939 were simply those in which seed sown earlier bore deadly fruit. Even the protracted and ghastly first World War was but an uncompleted episode that delayed rather than averted the end. What we still, now somewhat anachronistically, call "modern history" can most meaningfully be said to have begun also in Paris on March 1, 1871: on that occasion conquering Germans entered the city to symbolize their victory in the Franco-Prussian War. The humiliating peace that ended this struggle consolidated the German Empire, led to the establishment of the Third French Republic, and defined the power struggle that would culminate in the blitzkrieg of 1940.

Few years have seen such important changes in the Western world as those around 1870. With the consolidation of a host of petty states into the modern kingdoms of Italy and Germany, the abolition of slavery and the establishment of the principle of the indissoluble union in the United States, the abolition of serfdom in Russia, and the elimination of the Vatican as a temporal political power with the absorption of the Roman States into Italy, four of the most influential hangovers from the Middle Ages had at last been eliminated at the very time that new inventions and improving industrial techniques vastly increased Western productive capacity.

The industrialization and centralization of the European economy spurred a new drive to control both sources of raw materials and captive markets for manufactured goods. England, France, Spain had already held and largely lost vast colonial empires. The Monroe Doctrine and Napoleon III's misadventure in Mexico discouraged dreams of re-establishing European political control of the Americas. The dynamic nations, prattling about "the white man's burden," turned, therefore, with new vigor to the division of heretofore generally inaccessible Africa and the South Seas and a less successful effort to appropriate China. While European nations had for centuries held stations on the African coast, the parceling out of the mysterious interior did not get fully underway until Germany and Italy were able to join France, England, and Belgium in grubstaking claims.

Concurrently with this change in the political complexion of the Western world, two important new doctrines had assumed the character of modern religions in providing motivation and direction for the change. Darwin's fastidiously scientific theories about natural selection and "the survival of the fittest" were vulgarized into a new defense for laissez-faire policies and predatory economic imperialism, while the Utopian dreams of library-haunting Karl Marx were to provide illiterate "have-nots" with their most effective rallying cry in a world of imperialist exploitation.

Casting about for a convenient label for this Age of Paris

in the history books of the future, one is struck by the pertinence of the word *irresponsible*. There had been irresponsible ages and rulers before, of course, but never had irresponsibility been able to manifest itself on such a global scale as during the nineteenth-century search for plunder and the twentieth-century convulsions over the distribution and management of this plunder. This irresponsibility reached its horrifying climax in the negotiations after the first World War, during which European powers sought to evade obligations accepted under pressure and the United States turned its back on the League of Nations, which offered the sole faint hope for preventing the repetition of past mistakes on a more cataclysmic scale, because our nation felt that it could retain its chastity only by shunning depraved foreigners and practicing a repressive prohibition at home.

The perfect symbols for this age of irresponsibility are the self-ordained aristocrats in F. Scott Fitzgerald's *The Great Gatsby*, who, as narrator Nick Carraway says, "retreated into their vast carelessness and left others to clean up the mess that they had made," while dreamers like Gatsby found only disillusionment and death awaiting them. In 1939 those remnants of the West that had not succumbed to some form of authoritarianism awoke at last to discover that with Czechoslovakia gone and Spain gone, too, a few days later, evasions eventually caught up with one and one must either accept responsibilities or capitulate to ruthless totalitarianism.

The decision to resist came nearly too late—had come too late defeatists suspected in the black days of 1940. Over nearly all the serious fiction of the late thirties hangs the overpowering shadow of the conviction that Paris and the world it provided with a cultural focal point would not rise again. Even the popular Kern and Hammerstein song spoke of remembering rather than regaining the lost world. The incredible defense of Britain, Hitler's staggering miscalculation in dividing his forces to attempt to subjugate Russia, the defeat of the fascist powers, and the subsequent fumbling attempts to move toward a new world under a threat of atomic destruction that could not be swept under the rug were in the unforeseeable future when the books that I will discuss were written, and about all of these books is an air of threnody for "civilized" man.

During the last days of this era of what seemed the suicide of individualism, each of three great American novelists, who have subsequently shared the supreme international distinction of winning the Nobel Prize, published one of his most ambitious novels. Curiously, the growing perspective of a quarter of a century allows us to see that in *The Hamlet, The Grapes of Wrath,* and *For Whom the Bell Tolls,* Faulkner, Steinbeck, and Hemingway made their outstanding contribution to the social novel.

This term, "social novel," needs explanation because almost all fiction dramatizes the relationship between the individual and society, and there is no accepted definition for the term. Generally, it has been applied to novels with a purpose or thesis, but again it is difficult to imagine a serious—or even readable—novel without some controlling thesis. In order to focus upon a specially interesting group of novels, I use the term in a very limited sense. By "social novel," I mean a work that is so related to some specific historical phenomena that a detailed knowledge of the historical situations is essential to a full understanding of the novel at the same time that the artist's manipulation of his materials provides an understanding of why the historical events involved occurred. The events may, like those connected with the Spanish Civil War or the Okie migration, be specifically indentifiable, or they may be invented to typify kinds of occurrences like strikes or lynchings that pose grave social problems.

The event need not have occurred close to the time of the writing if the novel deals—like Robert Penn Warren's

*Night Rider*—with a force—like twentieth-century terrorist groups—still active when the novel appeared, especially if the novelist (like Warren) draws upon a background of his own experiences. I am not concerned, however, with that diverting anomaly, the "historical novel," which purports to re-create the surface appearance of the glamorous past. Nor do I consider the kind of case study like the Utopian novel [2] in which an unlikely tale is concocted to communicate the author's vision of the good society. The novels I treat are most likely to be confused with such plump clannish chronicles as Stephen Longstreet's hard-bound soap opera *Decade: 1929-1939*, in which the interminable petty bickerings of a self-centered family are occasionally interrupted by cries like, "Goodness, the market has crashed!" or "I see poor Austria has been raped by the Nazi beast," to lend an unwarranted air of social history.

The novels that I will discuss are rather of special interest, not only to literary enthusiasts, but also—as Nelson M. Blake points out—to social scientists and anyone else interested in deepening his knowledge of the world.[3] When these novels are read in conjunction with histories of the period they portray, the two kinds of work shed reciprocal light on each other and deepen our awareness that truth cannot be glimpsed from a single perspective.

There is likely to be little quarrel that *The Grapes of Wrath* is both Steinbeck's grandest achievement and one of the outstanding works of social fiction of its era, however we define "social novel" and limit the era. A best seller for two years after its publication, this saga of dispossessed Oklahomans seeking a new start against overwhelming odds in California has, unlike most best sellers, remained one of the most widely read works of American fiction. Despite some detractors, and irrelevant criticism based on Steinbeck's failure to produce another work of comparable stature, Alexander Cowie's judgment, in *The Rise of the American Novel*, that in *The Grapes of Wrath* "most of the new features" in fiction "that have any value find a brilliant and powerful synthesis" [4] has remained the definitive appraisal.

Critics disagree as to which of Hemingway's novels should be called "best," but his most devoted student, Carlos Baker, considers *For Whom the Bell Tolls*, Hemingway's longest and most complex work and the most important literary monument to one of the most portentous events of the thirties, the Spanish Civil War, "a genuinely great novel." [5] Along with Picasso's Guernica mural, Hemingway's novel of Spain in agony, culminating in the description of the Calvary of El Sordo's guerilla band, achieves one of the highest purposes of social fiction as it bares the sufferings of a still largely primitive people that lie behind the headlines, about the destructive capacity of the mechanized force let loose upon these people.

The inclusion of Faulkner's *The Hamlet* in this trio is likely to be most controversial. Almost ignored by reviewers of a period that was just beginning to discover Faulkner, the novel was dismissed for years as simply a collection of related pseudo-folk tales about Southern grotesques. After Peter Lisca and others demonstrated *The Hamlet*'s organic unity, it was viewed principally as a kind of modern myth of man's productive and destructive capacities.[6] Without wishing to deny the mythological implications of Faulkner's extraordinary story, I would also like to argue for a more balanced approach that reveals it, too, as a painstaking and accurate revelation of the Mississippi state of mind that not only reflects much thinking in the modern (and ancient) world, but that has been specifically responsible for many of the continuing tensions and tragedies that have resulted in the United States from the racial situation and the nation's slowness in taking appropriate steps to remedy it.

All the books of Faulkner's Yoknapatawpha saga are

social novels in the sense that they shed psychological light on conspicuous events in recent Southern and general American history: the decline of the Bourbons (*The Sound and the Fury*), the degeneration of the yeoman (*As I Lay Dying*), the growth of native fascism (*Light in August*), the repetition of old errors when the oppressed rise to avenge themselves (*Absalom, Absalom!*). I think, however, that *The Hamlet* is the most important social novel of the group because it deals with the behavior that has had the strongest impact, not just in making Mississippi the most backward and stagnant state in the nation, but also in hindering the progress of the whole country and making the United States appear ridiculous through the presence in Congress of such megalomaniacs as Senator James K. Vardaman, Senator Theodore Bilbo, and Representative John Rankin. *The Hamlet* depicts the exploitation of the ignorant and paranoid "redneck" by utterly amoral persons motivated by a gross lust for personal power.

An examination of the backgrounds of these three novels, I hope to show, aids in understanding the fatal forces at work during the dying era. By focusing upon the political forces reflected in *The Hamlet*, the sociological theorizing culminating in *The Grapes of Wrath*, and the literary isolationism that finds its most dignified artistic embodiment in *For Whom the Bell Tolls*, I hope that it can be demonstrated that the three American writers of the period whom the world has subsequently most highly honored, present—probably quite unintentionally—in books published at the summit of their careers a living monument to some of the most characteristic forces that brought their world to its death throes.

The three novels upon which I concentrate were not, of course, the only social fiction to appear in 1939 and 1940, but the authors whose names had become most strongly identified during the two preceding decades with the social novel contributed disappointingly little during the last months of the dying age. Although Sinclair Lewis had as recently as 1935, in *It Can't Happen Here*, written seriously if somewhat woodenly of the threat of fascism to the United States and had even later worked intermittently on novels about labor leadership and the Negro problem, his contribution to fiction during the critical year in which the long-threatened collapse occurred was *Bethel Merriday*, an affectionate confection about a stage-struck young Connecticut girl who learns to become a trouper. Dorothy Canfield Fisher took over from Lewis the initiative against fascism; but *Seasoned Timber*, which tells of the conflict that ensues in the summer of 1937 when a wealthy trustee wills at least a million dollars to a down-at-the-heels secondary school in Vermont if it will exclude Jews, makes the incipient native fascists such thoroughly repugnant creatures that they are no more impressive than the cardboard figures in shooting galleries.

John Dos Passos' first novel after the completion of the *U. S. A.* trilogy was an enormous disappointment, not because it marked the beginning of the author's retreat to conservatism, but because the main character in *Adventures of a Young Man* never undergoes any change that sustains interest in the episodic recital of his career from his early misadventures as counselor at a boys' camp to his death at the hands of the Loyalist forces he attempts to aid in the Spanish Civil War. The whole story is told in the brief second chapter in which young Glenn Spotswood unprotestingly takes the blame for an act of childish brutality that he had protested but that had been attributed to him by the victim that he had tried to save. Glenn is simply the traditional fall guy, the "patsy" of Tennessee Williams's *Camino Real*, the "sad sack" of World War II cartoon fame. He is, as a ten-year-old pointed out to Thomas Parkinson, what some of the epic heroes of the past were, simply stupid,[7] so that his death at the hands of his supposed friends is not tragic or even pathetic, but inevitable. His goose has been cooked from the day he emerged in print as a lisping babe.

The "strike" novel had flourished during the thirties, but two aspiring writers failed to make significant additions to the genre at the end of the decade. Albert Maltz, recently converted from play-writing to tale-telling, might have provided a chilling and momentous account of the rise of the fascistic, strike-breaking Black Legion in the Midwest in his *The Underground Stream*, but he became so obsessed with trying to provoke sympathy for one martyred Communist organizer that he never allowed his other characters to come to life. Elliott Paul was scarcely a new writer, but *The Stars and Stripes Forever* was his first "social novel" in a decade. Unfortunately Paul, who had been driven back to the United States after long expatriation only by the Spanish Civil War, appeared to tire of his complicated account of a strike before he finished it, so that what might have been a provocative account of the struggle between paternalistic employers and employees concerned about the recognition of their dignity as individuals, ends in a violent apocalypse that leaves the paternalist curdled into fascist "sitting on top of the world." Paul's cynicism is understandable in view of his own crushing experiences on a small Balearic island, but his novel seems the result of personal outrage rather than detached observation. He was probably well-advised in subsequently abandoning the novel and devoting himself to the popular personal reminiscences that had begun with his *Life and Death of a Spanish Town*.

Two writers who had functioned as the social conscience of the early thirties failed to produce even as satisfactory visions of the late thirties as Paul, because of the artificiality and thinness of the books in which they attempted to deal with two of the most distressing manifestations of native American fascism: lynching and anti-Semitism.

*Trouble in July* was Erskine Caldwell's first novel in four years, most of which he had spent traveling with photographer Margaret Bourke-White collecting material for collaborative essays on rural Southerners and Czechoslovakians. Although lynching was still a serious problem when he wrote (there were seven authenticated lynchings in 1938), the characters in *Trouble in July* are such improbable caricatures that their plight contributes nothing to an understanding of the tense situation in the South. The Negro characters are so kind, guileless, and pure, and the whites so vicious and irrational, that the complexity of the situation disappears in a collection of unconvincing clichés.

In *Tommy Gallgaher's Crusade*, James T. Farrell focused much more sharply on the dangerous effects of anti-Communist and anti-Semitic preaching than Caldwell had on the forces motivating lynchings. Farrell deals with a rabble-rousing Father Moylan, who might as well have been outrightly named Father Coughlin after the enormously successful "radio priest," whose hatred for the New Deal led him to a defense of fascists and warnings against the conspiracies of international Jewry until he was silenced by the outbreak of the war. Farrell's novel characterizes one of the followers that Coughlin attracted as lazy, surly, hostile to his superiors, relieving his frustrations by threatening inoffensive Jews and breaking up small radical rallies. The possibly fifteen-thousand word tract was deservedly praised as a devastatingly accurate portrait of the incipient fascist, but the work was so slender that Tommy's situation was not even completely enough dramatized to make its significance clear to those not already aware of the menace of the rabble rouser. Farrell's book appears to have been written, not like *The Grapes of Wrath*, to enlighten and warn an uncomprehending public, but to capitalize upon the widespread dislike for Coughlin and his ilk by selling what should have been an inexpensive pamphlet as an extravagantly printed book.

Two books by relatively new novelists that shared the 1939 American Booksellers' Awards with *The Grapes of Wrath* were of unusual significance. Chosen as the "most original" work was Dalton Trumbo's harrowing account of a multiple amputee veteran of World War I, *Johnny Got His Gun,* while Elgin Groseclose's account of the persecution of the Armenians in *Ararat* was cited as "the booksellers' discovery." It is unfortunate that neither novel has continued to receive attention, for they are two of the most successful embodiments in American fiction of the warring philosophies of communism and Christianity that have inspired so many high-minded literary disasters. While Trumbo's novel suffers from the incorporation into it of too much unassimilated propaganda, its story remains harrowing, and it provides a more useful contrast with the outstanding social novels of its period than most defective works which suffer from the author's confused thinking and deficient inventiveness. *Ararat* powerfully illustrates, on the other hand, how traditional beliefs may still generate successful fiction. Surely it is curious to find that the two ends of the spectrum of twentieth-century faith found their most powerful dramatic embodiments in the hands of their most successful American exponents during the same brief period of the collapse of the world they sought to redeem; it is even more remarkably curious evidence of the catholicity of American booksellers' taste that such diametrically opposed books shared an award.

The two authors were not to repeat their success: Dalton Trumbo abandoned fiction for motion-picture scriptwriting after one more trivial and contrived story, and Elgin Groseclose withdrew into historical accounts that have scarcely been noticed. The two years under consideration here also marked the high-water point in the careers of the three principal novelists under consideration. Again, there is likely to be little dispute that Steinbeck has

never again equalled *The Grapes of Wrath;* one of
Faulkner's most ambitious undertakings, *A Fable,* lay far
in the future, but few find it the equal of *The Hamlet,*
which brought together some of the best tales that the
author had contrived during the thirties, which also saw
the publication of his most highly praised novels. While
many do consider Hemingway's *The Old Man and the Sea*
one of his outstanding works, it is technically a puny thing
beside the vast and organically sound architecture of *For
Whom the Bell Tolls.* The beginning of the forties marked
the beginning of a decline in the work of our most
distinguished social novelists.

Perhaps the most striking evidence, however, that some
kind of terminal had been reached was that the American
writer whose name had been for three decades most
conspicuously linked with the kind of social novel that he
could fairly be said to have invented decided suddenly in
1939 to abandon his efforts to reform the world and to
retreat into reminiscence.

Only a few years previously Upton Sinclair had run for
governor of California on his E.P.I.C. (End Poverty in
California) platform, and within the immediately preceding years of 1937 and 1938 he had ground out tracts about
current events with his accustomed vigor: *No Pasaran!,* his
contribution to the Spanish Republican cause; *Flivver
King* and *Little Steel,* exposés of the inner corruption of
two of America's most powerful industries. Sensing, however, that an end was coming, Sinclair decided to withdraw
from his characteristically active involvement in affairs and
to look back over the era through which he had lived,
beginning with a story of the machinations culminating in
the first World War. With almost uncanny aptitude, he
chose for the first book of the sequence that was to win
more readers than his crusading novels of the thirties a title
that is a slogan for the period: *World's End.*

Sinclair was to devote the next decade—sitting out the

despicable but predictable catastrophe of World War II—to shaping his legend of Lanny Budd, incredibly handsome and gifted bastard of a munitions king and an international beauty queen, whose charm and vigor won him the right to sit in on the making of history. Although Sinclair chose to fashion his fable, not around a young fighter from the ranks, but rather a fairy-tale prince who fulfilled everyman's dream of being young, dashing, and wealthy, the Lanny Budd books cannot simply be lightly written off as appealing fantasies. Necessarily superficial, they are still spiced with an old campaigner's vigorous ironies about the foibles of the powerful, a generous dose of slyly inserted propaganda for the liberal causes he had long espoused, and venomously apt portraits of the great of the era. There are few pleasanter ways to supplement the reading of the history of the early twentieth century than to follow at the same time the fast-moving adventures of the graceful and impetuously idealistic young American superman through whom Upton Sinclair allows the reader to indulge his desire to play a role in shaping world affairs.

This was a period for such voluminous reminiscence. Posthumously, Thomas Wolfe's vast account of the struggles of the uncompromising individualist appeared in *The Web and the Rock* and *You Can't Go Home Again*. In France, Jules Romains's chronicle of twentieth-century French history reached its climax in *Verdun*, the story of the central struggle in World War I, just in time for the novel to serve as an epitaph for a Paris vanquished at last in World War II. Josephine Herbst was bringing her multivolumed, socially conscious cliff-hanger about the fragmentation of the tight world of an American family to a conclusion in *Rope of Gold*. Few novels, however, capture the recklessly irresponsible flavor of the age with the authenticity of Sinclair's first chronicle of Lanny Budd. The irrepressible veteran hit precisely the right note to tell the story of the Age of Paris. Although the action whirls occasionally to Connecticut, the British countryside, a

German feudal estate, the Côte d'Azur—the real world of the people who mattered in the *belle epoque* early in the century—it centers around Paris, capital of the arts and intrigues of the age; and as befits a people who tried to bring to life their good and wicked dreams without recking consequences, it is a superficially charming and fundamentally sordid fantasy.

Significantly, too, no beginning novelists emerged during 1939 and 1940 to occupy the places that Upton Sinclair and Sinclair Lewis had once held. The proletarian literary movement, one of the most productive sources of new social novelists in the middle thirties, had just about run its course by 1939. A novelist like Pietro di Donato, who brought a fresh and vigorous viewpoint to the American social scene, was a victim of the very irresponsibility that destroyed the age, and even Richard Wright was diverted from developing as an artist. The only beginning social novelist later to exceed his original promise was Robert Penn Warren, an academician, who championed a vastly different approach to the creative arts from his bumptious and often slapdash predecessors in social analysis.

It should finally be noted as of far more than passing curiosity that these same years saw, too, the publication by the world's outstanding experimental writer of his protracted efforts to produce the monumental embodiment of all the new literary techniques that the Age of Paris had fathered. After the long awaited appearance in 1939 of James Joyce's dream history of everybody, *Finnegans Wake*, it was clear that if there was still to be an *avant garde*, it would have to move in a new direction. It is thus fair to say that 1939 and 1940 marked not only the end of an era in social and political history, but the end of a literary generation, especially in the creation of the social novel.

New writers would also need to appear if a new age emerged from the ashes.

## 2　A TROUBLED SECTION—
## "A LITTLE SWEETENING
## FOR THE CHAPS"

IN TREATING Faulkner's *The Hamlet* as a social novel, my
intention is not to draw, as John Cullen delightfully does
in *Old Times in the Faulkner Country*, explicit parallels
between real people and Faulkner's characters. Nor do I
intend to construct a picture of Mississippi at the turn of
the century from clues in the novel. Rather I wish to
confront the historical record of the period with Faulkner's
portrayal in the novel of human beings dramatizing their
values through their actions. This confrontation shows, I
believe, how the "Snopesism" that reached the peak of its
power during the decade of the depression arose from the
political situation that developed gradually in Mississippi
after Reconstruction and reached its climax just after the
turn of the century about the time that Flem Snopes
began his rise.

To support the validity of this effort, I call upon
Faulkner himself, who said during his visit to Japan, "In
my country, an artist is nothing. Nobody pays attention to
him. . . . In my country, instead of asking the artist what
makes children commit suicide, they go to the Chairman
of General Motors and ask him. That is true. If you make a
million dollars, you know all the answers." [1] But this
cynical outburst means that Faulkner did believe that we
might ask the artist. He also said during these talks at
Nagano that he loved his country enough "to want to cure

its faults" by shaming and criticizing it. He felt that the writer "should not be just a 'recorder' of man—he should give man some reason to believe that man can be better than he is." [2] The novelist must thus go beyond "the facts," but this does not mean that he necessarily ignores them. *The Hamlet* certainly reflects archetypal patterns of behavior, but to treat the novel exclusively as a kind of universal myth is to miss some of its vital qualities. Cleanth Brooks observes that more than any other novel of Faulkner's, this first volume of the Snopes saga introduces us to "a strange and special world," [3] but this world is no fantasy. It is the Mississippi of the half century between Reconstruction and the Great Depression.

I remember, as what Faulkner would call a "chap," studying civics in a large Northern city and developing from election returns a concept of Mississippi as monolithically single-minded, a place where the most unswerving kind of conformity was not demanded, but simply taken for granted as the price of existence. I had to go to Mississippi to discover the error in this concept. It is correct, of course, to the extent that "White Supremacy" continues to be almost universally the fundamental tenet of local faith. As very recent events show, those foolhardy enough to challenge this tenet find the defenders of the tradition still willing to turn the state into a bloody battleground.

Mississippians, however, even when embattled, can agree among themselves on little except the divinely ordained inferiority of nonwhites. If the racial issue did not necessitate an uneasy united front, Mississippi would probably be even more politically paralyzed by irreconcilable sectional cleavages than such sites of urban-rural friction as New York and Illinois. The causes of this disunity go far back into the history of the state, little known to outsiders because delving into Mississippi affairs has little appeal for the fastidious.

At the time of the Civil War, the state was just emerging from frontier conditions. Its greatest growth had occurred between 1830 and 1840 when migrants from the Eastern part of the South tripled the 1817 population of 70,000. This was the period during which—as Faulkner describes in the violent pages of *Absalom, Absalom!* and the interchapters of *Requiem for a Nun*—plantations and communities were violently wrested from the virgin soil. By 1860, too, the state boasted some of the wealthiest citizens of the nation.

The Civil War prostrated the state; many of the able-bodied men who had directed its growth were dead or discredited. With the abolition of slavery, the plantation system needed a vast reorganization, for which the state had neither the money, the energy, nor the objective intelligence. Away from the regions along the Mississippi and Yazoo Rivers, the thin, exploited soil was already showing signs of exhaustion.

Mention of the soil brings us to the outstandingly important fact that Mississippi is divided into three quite varying sections. Most of the power in the early days of the state centered in the rich Delta, lying between and along the Mississippi and the Yazoo. Here were located the ante bellum plantations that have assumed mythical dimensions as a result of such latter-day extravaganzas as the Natchez pilgrimage. The Delta had early assumed control of state politics and would ever be reluctant to relinquish it.

In another world from the prosperous, flood-prone Delta is the so-called Piney Woods region of Southern Mississippi, a sparsely settled lumbering area with poor soil, whose principal products have been the lumbering brutes who have given the University of Mississippi winning football teams and Senator Theodore Bilbo. Most of the poverty-stricken population of the Piney Woods region is white; the Negroes are largely concentrated in the Delta.

East of the Delta, north of the Piney Woods, rise the "red clay hills," on the western edge of which is Oxford, long Faulkner's home and model for the Jefferson of his Yoknapatawpha saga. This land of "rednecks" combines the worst features of the other two sections: the pretentiousness and aristocratic arrogance of the Delta (there is even a Natchez-like pilgrimage in Holly Springs, thirty miles north of Oxford) with the poverty, exhausted soil, and bigotry of the Piney Woods. This combination is immortally captured in that scene in *The Hamlet* in which Ab Snopes grinds horse dung into Major de Spain's hundred-dollar French rug (p. 17).[4] Clearly this ill-favored region, which has fewer Negroes than the Delta, but more than the Piney Woods, holds the balance of power between the fastness of the Bourbon traditionalists and the marches of the illiterate barbarians.

After Mississippi regained its statehood in 1870, a power struggle began. The radical Republican machine managed to force Negro rule on Mississippi longer than on most of the South, but it was at last supplanted in 1876, largely through the diplomatic manipulations of Lucius Quintus Cincinatus Lamar, a man dedicated to his own advancement, who shrewdly succeeded in inserting himself into the confidence of even suspicious Northerners. Lamar provided almost the only powerful link between the Old and the New Mississippi. Born in 1825 in Georgia (from which many influential Mississippians had migrated), he had even served in the legislature of his home state before moving with his father-in-law, Augustus Baldwin Longstreet, distinguished jurist and author of *Georgia Scenes*, who had become chancellor of the newly established University of Mississippi.

Lamar soon projected himself with enthusiasm into the affairs of his adopted home and distinguished himself as the author of its secession ordinance. Soon proving physically unable to endure combat, he became the Confederate emissary to Imperial Russia. After the war he returned to teach law at the University of Mississippi, from which strategic spot on the boundary between hills and Delta, he exercised such remarkable powers of political manipulation that he became the first Democrat elected to the state legislature since the end of the War, in the very year (1872) that the Amnesty Act restored full political privileges to disfranchised Southerners.

Subsequently, he became the first white United States Senator from Mississippi since the hostilities, and he capped his career by achieving the greatest national distinctions for which a former rebel could have hoped—a place first in Cleveland's cabinet as Secretary of the Interior and at last an appointment as associate justice of the Supreme Court. Albert D. Kirwan says with unquestionable accuracy that at the time White rule was restored in Mississippi, Lamar's "approval was almost sufficient to guarantee election—his disapproval, to insure defeat." [5] Precisely thirty-five years later, in 1911, James Kimble Vardaman was in the same position; but he was by no stretch of the imagination Lamar's heir. Indeed "The Great White Chief," as Vardaman was fondly known, consolidated his power by crushing at last the spokesman of the postwar "Bourbon" party that Lamar founded. The story of Mississippi politics in the year that Faulkner's *The Hamlet* illuminates is the story of the shift of power from Lamar to Vardaman, as the story of the novel is that of the shift of power from Will Varner to Flem Snopes.

To understand what happened, we must first realize that the late nineteenth-century Bourbons in Mississippi were not identical with the aristocratic, flamboyant Bourbon planters who controlled the state before the Civil War. As Kirwan points out in *Revolt of the Rednecks*, those who stubbornly held to the past and refused to pay lip service to the war amendments "were few in Mississippi politics and they exercised little influence" (p. 8). The new Bourbons were not unsophisticated planters obsessed by dreams like

Thomas Sutpen's of establishing baronial fiefdoms, but, like Lamar, principally corporation lawyers who identified themselves with the aggressive railroads that were responsible for what small economic progress the state made before the end of the century. They inherited the Bourbon name, however, because like their predecessors they fancied themselves the stable and responsible element in the state, in opposition to the poor, dirty, and largely illiterate hill farmers who were beginning to cry for relief.

Agricultural reforms were hard to achieve in Mississippi because the Bourbons equated any effort to break with the Democratic party that they controlled, with a threat to continued white dominance in the state. The black menace was used to hold dissidents in line while ignoring their complaints. It was argued that only complete Democratic unity could prevent a resurgence of Black Republicanism; nor did these selfless leaders rely only on argument to protect the "rednecks" from potential folly. Every device for stuffing ballot-boxes and fixing returns was employed, and not only Negroes were lynched. In a notorious episode in Kemper County in 1877, Judge W. W. Chisholm, a white independent who had been a Republican, two of his teen-aged children, and a British friend were shot as they fled from a jail that a mob had set on fire.[6] Control of the state was almost completely in the hands of the Executive Committee of the Democratic Convention, which was in turn managed by Lamar and his fellow Senator, the corporation lawyer James Z. George, who was apparently responsible for the provisions in the Mississippi Constitution of 1890 that at last "solved" the problem of formally disfranchising the Negro—the poll-tax and the "understanding" of the State Constitution clauses. Cleanth Brooks notes that "the Negro has hardly any part" in Faulkner's *The Hamlet*, and indeed, during this period, Negroes played no effective role in the political life of the state.

The new constitution, which did cut the actual vote in

the state nearly in half, served, however, only to further dissension among the whites. By 1890 it had become apparent, for one thing, that the Delta, while monopolizing political power, was not paying anything like its proportionate share of state taxes. The campaign of 1891 between incumbent Senator George and Ethelbert Barksdale, representative of the insurgent farmers, for electors was one of the bitterest and most violent in the state's history.

The defeat of the farmers is generally attributed to Bourbon control of the party machinery, but it is doubtful that affairs in Mississippi can be thus rationally explained. Another element that played an enormous part is explained in Kirwan's summary of the campaign in 1892 between the Bourbon candidates for Congress and the Populists, to whom the farmers had turned:

> [The Populists] charged that "the Bourbon Democrats" had foisted [the franchise provisions of the Constitution] on the people in an attempt to curtail the privilege of voting.
>
> The Democrats answered the challenge with the old rallying cry of white supremacy. They accused the Populists of favoring Negro suffrage . . . .
>
> To all the clamor which the Populists made for reform, the Democrats answered that there were some things more important than reforms in the economy. A Populist victory, they warned, would result in Negro supremacy and the degradation of Southern womanhood. (*Revolt of the Rednecks*, p. 95)

The "things" that mattered more than reform were, of course, those elements of the "Mississippi tradition" of which the Bourbons considered themselves the sole defenders; as long as they could convince the voters to accept the Bourbon candidates as the defenders of whites against blacks, the reform candidates could never win by insisting upon debating economic issues on their own merits. *The Hamlet* suggests through the portrayal of characters like

Henry Armstid and Mink Snopes and WallStreet Panic Snopes that many of Mississippi's "peasants" were paranoid; here art follows reality.

As if to test the hypothesis that the farmer's party could achieve victory only when it found a spokesman who could beat the Bourbons at their own game by outshouting them, James K. Vardaman appeared on the scene.

Vardaman has lent his name to two of Faulkner's most repulsive characters—the feeble-minded youngest Bundren child in *As I Lay Dying*, and one of the loathesome Snopes twins who try to agitate the man who may be their grandfather into a stroke in *The Town*. Although Vardaman died in 1930, he still lingers in our commercial folklore as the prototype for Al Capp's Senator Phogbound and other mass-media solons. He injected new drama into political campaigning by appearing in Mississippi's numerous hamlets in an eight-wheeled lumber cart drawn by several pairs of white oxen, dressed all in white, with his dark hair falling down to his shoulders, and demanding that the dangerous practice of educating Negroes cease.

He was of the post-Civil War generation, having been born in 1861 to parents who had migrated from Mississippi to Texas, but who returned home after the conflict. He grew up and attended public schools—like the one I. O. Snopes conducts in *The Hamlet*—in Yalobusha County, directly below Lafayette County, where Faulkner lived, and only a few miles from the Frenchman's Bend country. When only twenty-one, Vardaman qualified for the bar and set up practice in Winona, a seedy county seat, strategically located on the road between Memphis and Jackson that forms the boundary between the Delta and the hills.

Soon he was editing the community newspaper, and in 1890—just as Flem Snopes progressed from the hamlet to Jefferson—Vardaman moved into the Delta to the flourishing city of Greenwood, which he soon began to represent in the state legislature. In 1895 he turned up as a candidate for governor, but withdrew for obscure reasons a month before the nominating convention. Since he had returned from the Spanish-American War a hero, however, he was less easy to deal with in 1899, when the last election was held in which the state convention nominated the candidate for governor. When he saw, however, during the first night's balloting that he could not muster the needed strength, he, along with other contenders, withdrew in favor of the incumbent's candidate.

The situation changed vastly, however, when by political maneuverings that are still not clear, a law was passed over Delta opposition providing for a statewide party primary to replace the scandal-ridden conventions. Vardaman was one of the two candidates to achieve the largest number of votes in the first primary; in the run-off, the newspapers observed that the fight was between "the conservative business element of the state," represented by an old Confederate soldier, and the upstart Vardaman (*Revolt of the Rednecks*, p. 159). But instead of arguing "issues," as his predecessors had when seeking vainly to unseat the Bourbons, Vardaman went to the people with dramatic speeches on the racial issue, arguing against education for Negroes and calling for repeal of the Fourteenth and Fifteenth amendments to the federal Constitution. Even the opposition agreed that Vardaman owed his victory to the revival of the white supremacy question and the new primary law which allowed him to exercise his magnetism directly on the kind of backwoods audience that buys the spotted horses in *The Hamlet*.

Vardaman's greatest tests came, however, during his campaigns for the Senate. Senators were still elected indirectly, but in Mississippi the candidates had since 1890 been nominated in the party primary. Vardaman made his first attempt at a senate seat in 1908 when he opposed incumbent John Sharp Williams in a campaign that featured—particularly as the principal issue in the only face-to-face debate between the contenders at Meridian on July 4, 1907—Vardaman's proposal for repealing the Constitutional amendments. So close was the election that Williams, the Delta planter, despite his organizational support, won by only 648 votes. Even while hailing the victory, the Bourbon press saw trouble coming.

It was not long arriving. The Bourbons had been able to hold on by the narrow margin that they did only because they had been able to maintain the illusion that they were the friends of all whites against the blacks. At Christmas, 1909, Mississippi's other senator died suddenly. Since the primary to replace him would not be held until 1911, the legislature had a free hand in naming his successor. As Kirwan says, "a contest was precipitated which was to have tremendous consequences on the politics of the state" (p. 191). Vardaman was pitted against Leroy Percy, a Delta planter and graduate of the University of the South at Sewanee, Tennessee. No more perfect candidate to maintain Bourbon tradition could have been found. Percy's son, William Alexander Percy, was later to produce, in *Lanterns on the Levee*, the book that articulates the Bourbon philosophy. Certainly Percy specified in this book the real issue in his father's campaigns against Vardaman, when he described the opponent as "a kindly, vain demagogue unable to think," who "looked like a top-notch medicine man" and stood for all that the elder Percy considered "vulgar and dangerous."[7] What none of the Bourbons would have said publicly during the campaigns, young Percy also admits in his book when he describes the poor whites to whom Vardaman appealed as "intellectually and spiritually . . . inferior to Negroes, whom they hate." He also describes them as a "gang of poor degenerates" that "lynch Negroes, that mistake hoodlumism for wit, and cunning for intelligence, that attend revivals and fight and fornicate in the bushes afterwards."[8] Vardaman's party believed that the Bourbons harbored such feelings, but the problem was to trap these canny politicians into expressing them so that they would be discredited in the eyes of those whose votes they sought.

There was no opportunity for a showdown during the legislative election, since the caucusing was secret. On the first ballot Vardaman led with 71 out of 170 votes; but he was finally defeated by Percy, after all other candidates had been forced out, six weeks later on the fifty-eighth ballot by 87 votes to 82. The caucus was marked by every conceivable illicit effort to influence votes, and its aftermath nearly led to the expulsion of Theodore Bilbo from the state legislature for his ambiguous role in some vote buying.

The voting ended in February, 1910. Although the next primary, for the full Senate term, would not be held for nearly two years (in November, 1911), campaigning between the same two men started almost at once. This time Vardaman could make his sensational appeals directly to the electorate, and Percy relied, as usual, on a counterappeal to people's conservatism. But the contest was tense and, as the title of subsection of *The Hamlet* points out, summers in Mississippi are long and hot. Tempers were already frayed by the long wrangle during the secret caucus. Violence sprang up again, centering around Bilbo, who was beaten into insensibility with a pistol by a man whom Bilbo had said was "a cross between a mongrel and a cur, conceived in a nigger graveyard at midnight, suckled by a sow, and educated by a fool." [9] Such episodes, however, served only to build up sympathy for the group that cast itself in the underdog role. The catastrophe for the Bourbons, for which W. A. Percy has provided the apt title "Sideshow Götterdämmerung," occurred on July 4, 1910.

As in previous elections, the candidates generally avoided confronting each other; but at Lauderdale Spring, near Meridian, on the holiday that always brought out the greatest crowds for political speechmaking, Percy was tricked into sharing the platform with Vardaman's lieutenant, Bilbo. Percy had promised his supporters to avoid personal attacks, but after listening to Bilbo, he lost control of himself and denounced both Vardaman and his ally. Kirwan reports in *Revolt of the Rednecks* that Percy said in part:

> It was not unusual for people to assemble, "out of idle curiosity," to view an unusual dwarf, a three-legged man, or a two-headed calf. Such exhibitions of physical monstrosities had no elevating effect; but the "exhibition of a moral monstrosity," such as was made in the person of Bilbo that day, "has a debasing and degrading effect." (p. 221)

The Bourbon press hailed the speech and reprinted it, but later had cause to regret this premature elation. All through Percy's diatribe, Bilbo had sat on a porch in a manner remarkably like Flem Snopes's, smiling quietly and listening, as Snopes did to old Will Varner.

But the greatest damage was done that same day at another flyspeck, Godbold Wells, where heckled by another crowd of bumpkins, Percy completely lost control and called his auditors "cattle" and "rednecks." These remarks turned the tide. As Kirwan reports, they "were adopted by the Vardaman following, and wherever Vardaman went to speak he was greeted by crowds of men wearing red neckties and was carried in wagons drawn by oxen" (p. 212). In the largest vote cast in Mississippi up to that time, Vardaman won a clear victory in the first primary with 76,000 votes to his opponents' combined 50,000. While many forces unquestionably influenced this surprising vote, the influence of Percy's ill-advised and widely circulated attacks upon "rednecks" is incalculable. The contempt of the Delta planter for "white trash" had been forced out into the open at last.

What must be observed with the same kind of horror that Faulkner's *The Hamlet* inspires, is that even this hurried account of thirty-five ugly years in Mississippi politics shows the lack of influence of significant economic and social issues in determining elections and the vast importance of irrational appeals to fears and prejudices, especially to the continuing fear of black domination at the time when the completely subjugated Negro posed little threat. How could the whole political history of a state hinge so much on irrationality and the opportunistic exploiting of it? History provides the record of what happened; but when we seek to understand the motives behind the events, we must turn to the intuitions of the perceptive novelist.

## ii

Despite extensive commentaries on Faulkner's Snopes novels, I cannot find that anyone has previously called attention to the way in which the geography of Frenchman's Bend, the community that gives *The Hamlet* its title, reproduces in miniature the physiological characteristics of the state of Mississippi. In the first paragraph of the novel, the setting is described as "a section of rich river-bottom country . . . hill-cradled and remote," and in the fantastic tale told of an idiot's romance with a cow, we find a fuller description of the relationship between valley and hill.

> A mile back he had left the rich, broad, flat river-bottom country and entered the hills—a region which topographically was the final blue and dying echo of the Appalachian mountains. . . . Now it was a region of scrubby second-growth pine and oak among which dogwood bloomed until it too was cut to make cotton spindles, and old fields where not even a trace of furrow showed any more, gutted and gullied by forty years of rain and frost and heat into plateaus choked with rank sedge and briers loved of rabbits and quail coveys, and crumbling ravines striated red and white with alternate sand and clay. (p. 196)

The story is thus set against the background of an area that harbors the same tensions as exist on a larger scale between the Delta and hills of the state.

Originally the hamlet was the site of the Old Frenchman's Place, "a tremendous pre-Civil War plantation." Much of the character of the people of the region is established by Faulkner's description of the reaction of three successive waves of settlers to this landmark.

Its builder had "quite possibly been a foreigner, though not necessarily French," but "all that remained of him was the river bed which his slaves had straightened for almost ten miles to keep his land from flooding." "Even his name was forgotten," Faulkner continues, "his pride but a legend about the land he had wrested from the jungle and tamed as a monument to that appellation which those who came after him . . . could not even read, let alone pronounce, and which now had nothing to do with any once-living man at all" (p. 4). The Old Frenchman thus typifies that generation which built Mississippi but vanished almost without record, leaving only a myth behind to be fleshed out as pilgrimage directors people the past or as Faulkner's Quentin Compson and his Canadian roommate at Harvard reconstruct the tale of Thomas Sutpen in *Absalom, Absalom!* But though he has become a myth, the old Frenchman still exerts, like the prewar Bourbons, a tangible influence on later generations through "the stubborn tale of money he buried somewhere about the place" (p. 4).

At the time the novel begins the plantation that the phantasmal old Frenchman wrested from the wilderness is a ruin in the receivership of Will Varner, as all of old Mississippi is a wasteland at the disposal of railroad builders. Varner is perhaps the most difficult character in the novel for the non-Mississippian to understand, for he seems as avaricious and amoral as the Snopeses; yet the author's sentiments about him are clearly ambiguous. This ambiguity is caught in a description that Faulkner attributes to Judge Benbow, one of Jefferson's patricians, "a milder-mannered man never bled a mule or stuffed a ballot box" (p. 5). Varner not only exploits Frenchman's Bend himself, but he exposes the hamlet and subsequently the whole county to the depredations of the Snopeses in an effort to protect his own holdings. Learning of the Snopeses' reputations as barn-burners, Varner acts first out of prudence and fear, as the postwar Bourbons did to prevent further havoc in an already prostrate state. Later, however, he tolerates Flem beyond the demands of prudence, conniving with him (as the Bourbons did at first with Vardaman) and even calling upon him to save daughter Eula's reputation. Yet despite this trafficking with evil, Varner is never denounced.

Through his treatment of Varner, Faulkner shows his own hand; for he must have felt—as L. Q. C. Lamar did—that there was little that one could do but compromise with evil if Mississippi was not to revert to wilderness. Varner occupied the same position with relationship to his tiny suzerainty that Lamar did to the state. Varner was "the fountainhead if not of law at least of advice and suggestion to a countryside which would have repudiated the term constituency if they had ever heard it. . . . He was a farmer, a usurer, a veterinarian" (p. 5). He owns most of the land in the region, although he is not essentially a planter, but a merchant, investor, and even inventor, who tries to keep the stagnant community alive. Lamar had been obliged to resort to fraud and demagoguery to restore Democratic control in Mississippi; but the region might have been in even worse condition without his efforts. Historians like Kirwan may justly be critical of Lamar's saving the region for obviously selfish reasons, and a modern novelist like Pat Frank can write Mississippi off in *Mister Adam* as an expendable site for nuclear tests, but William Faulkner couldn't—at least not back in the thirties when he was fashioning the early chapters in the

Snopes saga. Behind the books written during the period of his greatest literary activity lies a love of his native soil as passionate and irrational as that the narrator expresses at the end of Gogol's *Dead Souls*.

Will Varner from the viewpoint of one who cares about Mississippi has one powerful redeeming virtue. His efforts, like those of Lamar and his generation, are guided by a desire for the success that eluded the Frenchman and the older Mississippi, rather than for the glory that they sought. Varner tells another character, as he sits "against his background of fallen baronial splendor" in his flour-barrel seat, that he's "trying to find out what it must have felt like to be the fool that would need all this . . . just to eat and sleep in" (p. 7). The Varner who makes this statement is a tragic figure, for just as he is bewildered by the past, he is perplexed by the future. Of his many children, only two—a bellicose coward and a sensual animal—remain at home. He is trying to maintain some human order in a region where generally only those with less than normal human drives remain.

Small wonder, then, that he is willing to close his eyes to the inhuman qualities of Flem Snopes, who, as William Faulkner's brother John has said, is representative of a group which by usurping power made the old residents "aware for the first time of the value of human endeavour." [10] Snopes is, however, as both a fantastic vision of his besting the devil and his impotency suggest, not really human. He sees the ruined old Frenchman's place not as the source of wonder it is to Will Varner, but simply as something to be exploited in his drive for success. Flem belongs to the same breed as Vardaman and his creature Bilbo. Faulkner, who had good reason to hate Bilbo for ousting Murray Faulkner, William's father, from his post as Comptroller of the University of Mississippi during a vendetta against the state system of higher education in 1930, surely felt that Snopesism was monstrous and that

Frenchman's Bend had fallen into the hands of worse than fiends, who made their fortunes by preying upon the ignorance and passions of the "peasants" for whom he names the last section of *The Hamlet*, just as Vardaman and Bilbo preyed upon them in campaigns designed to inflame "White Supremist" sentiments.

The comparison between Snopesism and Vardamanism is most manifest, however, in the portrayal of the conflict that really serves to link together the superficially only casually related episodes of *The Hamlet*—Flem Snopes's effort to complete the subjugation of his environment by overcoming Ratliff, an itinerant sewing-machine salesman.

Ratliff is something far more than a detached observer who gets drawn into the affairs of Frenchman's Bend. The crucial statement about this apostle of modest progress occurs immediately before a conversation that he has with Will Varner about the gift of the Old Frenchman's place to Flem Snopes in return for Flem's marrying Varner's pregnant daughter Eula.

> [Varner] sat the old horse and looked down at Ratliff, the little hard eyes beneath their busy rust-colored brows glinting at the man who was a good deal nearer his son in spirit and intellect and physical appearance too than any of his own get. (p. 180)

Faulkner thus conceives of Ratliff as Varner's true heir; and if the region has any intellectual and spiritual future at all, it depends not upon Varner's apathetic and trouble-making children, but on Ratliff, who has stayed on in Mississippi, even though he, like Will Varner, has abilities that should assure his success elsewhere.

Through this intimation of the relationship between the two men, Faulkner suggests that the expedients to which the men of Lamar's generation yielded were dictated by their hopes for the future. Certainly if Flem Snopes is able to defeat Ratliff, the victim will not be just one man or one small community, but a way of life that some have struggled for generations to preserve.

This struggle that dominates the book first comes into focus when Ratliff, discussing Varner's son Jody's efforts to cope with the Snopeses, comments, "there aint but two men I know can risk fooling with them folks. And just one of them is named Varner, and his front name aint Jody." When Varner asks who the other is, Ratliff replies "pleasantly," "That aint been proved yet neither" (p. 31).

Shortly afterwards, Ratliff first "risks fooling" with the Snopeses by attempting to outwit Flem in a deal involving some apparently worthless goats. Ratliff does best Snopes to the extent of making Flem see "what it feels like" to burn up money, but he loses his profit on the transaction because he has not been cautious enough to discover before getting too deeply involved that Flem has no compunction about exploiting a feeble-minded relative. Whereas Ratliff would use his strength to protect society from being debased by the idiot, Flem will use his to exploit the idiot in victimizing society. This incident supports John Faulkner's attribution of his brother's hatred of Snopeses to their cruel treatment of the epileptic son of an old Oxford family.[11]

The incident also serves to draw the line between Ratliff and Snopes on the basis of their differing concepts of social responsibility and to establish also Ratliff's fatal weakness for acting too precipitately—perhaps even quixotically when his emotions are aroused. This shortcoming is noted by the compassionless Flem, who will be motivated in the future to triumph over this man who has bettered him. After the episode, Ratliff simply sends back to Varner the cryptic message, "It aint been proved yet neither" (p. 101).

The next round is Ratliff's. While Flem is off in Texas waiting for Eula's baby to grow enough to bring back to the hamlet, Ratliff uses his strength—as the Bourbon party did in the secret caucus—to frustrate Lancelot Snopes's vicious scheme to profit from alerting the hamlet's idly curious when his feeble-minded cousin is about to make love to a cow. Certainly by sending Vardaman to Washington, Mississippi provided the curious of the nation with a similarly edifying spectacle.

The next brush with Flem himself, however, produces more equivocal results. The episode of the sale of the spotted horses from Texas remarkably parallels the controversy about vote-buying during the secret caucus for the Mississippi senatorial nomination, since Flem Snopes (like Vardaman) never shows his hand directly, but allows his subalterns to bear the brunt of the ensuing litigation as Vardaman had Bilbo. Ratliff manages to preserve his honor, since he is not duped into buying one of the worthless monsters, but he is embarrassed—as the Bourbons were by counter-revelations during the lurid Bilbo trial—by being obliged to jump from his hotel window when one of the horses gets as far as his door, and he is obliged to see his friends suffer, while further incurring the wrath of the Snopeses for avoiding their trap, just as Percy roused Vardaman's enmity by failing to yield to a mandate of the people. Snopes, after all, by providing the "peasants" with an opportunity to buy the worthless horses, gave the public what it wanted.

Discussing the episode of the horse sale, Ratliff most fully articulates just what the struggle with the Snopeses means to him. Asked if he has returned to the pathetic Henry Armstid the money which his wife had earned weaving at night, Ratliff answers that he could have, but didn't, just as he had not, after the goat episode, burned a promissory note out of merely sentimental concern for a feeble-minded Snopes.

"I wasn't protecting a Snopes from Snopeses; I wasn't even protecting a people from a Snopes. I was protecting something that wasn't even a people, that wasn't nothing but something that dont want nothing but to walk and feel the sun and wouldn't know how to hurt no man even if it would and wouldn't want to even if it could, just like I wouldn't stand by and see you steal a meat-bone from a dog. I never made them Snopeses and I never made the folks that cant wait to bare their backsides to them. I could do more, but I wont. I wont, I tell you!" (p. 367)

Ratliff has no wish to be his brother's keeper. He is a sharp man in a business transaction. As he points out when he deprives the feeble-minded Snopes of the cow for which he has developed an infatuation, he acts because he is "stronger," not "righter" or "any better, maybe" (p. 227). What Ratliff wishes to maintain is an atmosphere in which decency can exist, as it surely cannot in a place where men watch quietly as another beats his wife, "their faces lowered as though brooding upon the earth at their feet" (p. 337), an atmosphere in which one can act spontaneously in behalf of what he believes in. The Snopeses prevent the maintenance of such an atmosphere, for a Flem, who can without showing any emotion at all quietly watch the man beat his wife, is constantly scheming to take advantage of any action by the remaining individuals who are not either cowed into abject submission or motivated by unfeeling calculation. Ratliff is especially angry that efforts to resist the Snopeses are especially handicapped by those so willing to "bare their backsides" to them that they will, like Mrs. Armstid after being victimized by the Snopeses, call Flem "right kind" when he buys her off with a nickel bag of candy, the same kind of "little sweetening for the chaps" (p. 362) that Vardaman and Bilbo so often handed out to the adoring throngs.

In their last contest, Flem Snopes is able to defeat even Ratliff. The whole transaction involving the sale of the old Frenchman's Place is remarkably similar to the Percy–Vardaman campaign of 1910. In this episode, Flem Snopes manages—without saying a word—to persuade Ratliff and some cohorts that there is indeed—as has long been rumored—money buried on the ruined estate, by salting the ruins with a bag of coins. Ratliff then offers to trade

Flem an interest in a lunch counter in Jefferson for the worthless property, so that Flem is last seen riding toward his next conquest, while Ratliff is left quite literally holding the bag.

Flem is able to trick Ratliff for two reasons that have important psychological implications. First, Ratliff, loyal to his native soil, has never been able to give up a baseless illusion that the ruins, which symbolize the mythical ante bellum land of wealth, still hold a buried fortune. His feelings reflect the persisting notion that there was still something for the present in the glamorous past that also led the Bourbon party in Mississippi, beset by upstarts, to turn to Leroy Percy, a candidate representative of traditional departed glories.

Ratliff, furthermore, would not have been victimized if he had not, because of his uncontrollable enthusiasm, failed to open at least one bag of the coins that he and his fellow excavators found. If he had, he would have discovered that the coins were minted after the Civil War and had to have been planted since the old Frenchman had vanished. Flem Snopes had found at last a way to exploit Ratliff's all too human weakness for acting in a moment of passionate enthusiasm without calculating all possible consequences. This is precisely what Bilbo did on July 4, 1910, when he succeeded in baiting Leroy Percy into his intemperate attack on "rednecks." A single slip sent Snopes riding toward Jefferson, Vardaman toward Washington.

Because of his sympathy for the defeated in this episode, Faulkner suggests that spontaneous outbursts of feeling must not be inhibited if man is not to be reduced to an unfeeling automaton. The vice of Snopesism is that its practitioners ape human traits without being fully human. They give man no reason to believe that he can be better than he is; rather they seek to destroy his distinguishing traits of compassion and spontaneity by exploiting them.

As Warren Beck writes in *Man in Motion*, a study of the Snopes trilogy, "Flem is, even more than Popeye [the grotesque criminal in *Sanctuary*], the modern automaton bred by materialism out of original crudeness." [12] The automatism of Faulkner's characters results not, however, from the dehumanizing forces of mechanization that many critics have decried, but from the peculiar political atmosphere in a state in which any true assertion of one's feelings might ruin one's prospects. Certainly the life in Frenchman's Bend is as primitive and unmechanized as life in an organized culture can be. Faulkner's novel sardonically points out that man cannot regain his spontaneity simply by fleeing the city and the machine.

Leadership in Mississippi had become by the early years of the twentieth century, not a matter of positive action to improve conditions, but a negative process of waiting for one's opponent to make a misstep or misstatement that one could pounce upon. Although Faulkner dealt with the period when the Vardamans and Snopeses first gained their power, the same situation prevailed in Mississippi in the 1930's. In fact, the state had slipped back into the hands of the Bilbo–Snopeses after seeming to have escaped from them in the twenties when a falling-out between Bilbo and Governor Lee Russell, a former henchman, restored the Bourbons to power. Bilbo, however, was able to sweep back into the governorship in 1927 in a campaign during which he literally threw bricks. This time he was determined to get control of higher education by moving the University of Mississippi, stronghold of Bourbonism, from remote Oxford to Jackson, where the governor could keep a close eye on it. Although by manipulating appointments to the State Board of Regents, he was able to precipitate a national scandal by firing the Chancellor of the University, forty-five faculty members, and a number of the administrative staff,[13] he was not successful in getting the University moved; and both his personal and professional reputation suffered badly. The depression found him in dire straits; he lost the "dream house" he was building, and by 1934 he was reduced to begging his Bourbon opponent, Senator Pat Harrison, for a humiliating post in the federal bureaucracy, until he had a chance to launch a campaign for a United States Senate seat in 1934.

A. Wigfall Green, Bilbo's scholarly biographer, who has long been intimately familiar with Mississippi politics, thinks that a "vibrant and colorful and popular" opponent in the 1934 Senate race would have "drawn and quartered Bilbo politically," [14] but the Bourbon mind seems never to learn. Against Bilbo, the traditionalists pitted Hubert Stephens, who as Green points out had already offended the "rednecks" by saying that "from the fetid filth of Mississippi politics as it exists today, offensive odors and tempests of disgrace have swept into every portion of the nation." [15] The Bourbons lost, and Bilbo regained the power that he was to wield until fatal illness and shrewder opposition caught up with him after World War II. Faulkner's *The Hamlet* presents, however, a precisely accurate portrait of the kind of figure that stood before the world—quite conspicuously in view of Bilbo's penchant for filibustering and making insulting statements—as a symbol of Mississippi at the end of the thirties.

Small wonder that a state whose ignorant prejudices made it putty in the hands of sharp and unscrupulous individuals motivated by a desire for self-aggrandizement often resembled an armed camp and that many of its able young people, like most of the children of Varner and of the owner of the barn in which the idiot hid his cow, left home and sometimes simply vanished. Certainly the atmosphere of constraint, not unique to Mississippi but fostered there by the unusual poverty, the fear of violence, and the threat of Negro resurgence, left the state almost completely in the hands of the kind of apathetic characters that gather around Varner's store in *The Hamlet*, the completely irrational and potentially psychotic buyers of spotted horses, and those greedy and cynical enough to observe this scene without revulsion and to attempt to advance themselves by callously exploiting the apathetic and the irrational.

Faulkner himself commented on this callous exploitation characteristic of the Snopeses, when he told an undergraduate audience at the University of Virginia that Flem "had to teach himself a certain shrewdness about people in order to make the money which he believed was the end of existence. . . . He probably understood all of his life [all] that he ever needed to understand." [16]

Surely the same thing could be said of Vardaman and Bilbo. It is hard to believe that it is purely coincidental that Faulkner began to publish the tales that were subsequently incorporated into *The Hamlet* at the very time that his family was most directly affected by Bilboism through the vengeful dismissal from the University of Mississippi of those officials that had dared stand in the path of the power hungry.

Thus while *The Hamlet* is not a story of Mississippi politics, it is a revelation of the inner workings of the culture that produced the politics. It gives the sensitive reader evidence that allows him to "Think Mississippian." Perhaps this is a dubious distinction, but it is one that can provide a vital perspective on some of the spasms that have for decades flowed over state boundaries to wrack our whole culture.

## 3  A TROUBLED NATION –
## "HOW NICE IT'S GONNA BE,
## MAYBE, IN CALIFORNIA"

DURING THE TWENTIES AND THIRTIES, large numbers of owners of small farms in the Southern and Southwestern states, as a result of the exhaustion of their soil and the continued depression of farm prices, lost their land to mortgage holders and became tenants or "share croppers." When the prolonged drought and accompanying severe dust storms of the 1930's resulted in the loss of a succession of crops, even the tenant farming system no longer worked and, in order to protect investments, the holding companies evicted the croppers and threw many small farms together into large ones that could be efficiently operated.

Instead of staying home and demanding some form of local relief, many evicted tenants took to the road like modern gypsies and toured the agricultural states in search of seasonal work. They were especially attracted to fertile and prosperous California. At first the large-scale West Coast farmers and canners encouraged the migration in order to assure themselves a supply of cheap and easily managed labor during the brief harvest seasons. Drought, evictions, and migration continued, however, longer than shortsighted manipulators had speculated, and in the late thirties the migration into California was getting out of control. Panicked, the Californians responded by enforcing an anti-migrant law which provided penalties for bringing the destitute into the state and by employing repressive police measures to control restlessness and labor agitation. This frightening and potentially explosive situation was eased only in the early 1940's when the increasing tempo of defense preparations provided an insatiable market for both agricultural and inexperienced factory labor.

All but the last chapter in this depressing history John Steinbeck illustrates in *The Grapes of Wrath*, through both the story of the migrant Joad family and the symbolic and polemical "inter-chapters" that depict the general situation and bring out the universal implications of the Joad story as it specifically illustrates aspects of the agricultural depression. Although the novel was attacked by many offended at the picture Steinbeck drew and though small inaccuracies can be found in the work—which is a novel and not a textbook—*The Grapes of Wrath* can be read, among other things, as a chillingly graphic portrayal of some shocking events of the thirties.

To treat the novel, however, as simply social history is to miss its significance. One seeking information about the period is better advised to turn to Steinbeck's "Their Blood is Strong," a collection of reports about conditions that he wrote for the *San Francisco News* as a result of firsthand observations of the migrant camps, and to the detailed and complementary studies by Carey McWilliams, then California Commissioner of Immigration and Housing, *Factories in the Fields* and *Ill Fares the Land*. I have already collected materials from these sources and others that describe events in the Dust Bowl and California during the thirties in *A Companion to "The Grapes of Wrath*," and it would be idle to repeat this factual background of the novel. I am interested in this study in the novel not as a mirror—however accurate—but as a creative vision that helps us to understand how the events it depicts came about.

Steinbeck's novel has actually been more frequently attacked as art than as propaganda. It has been charged that it lacks artistic unity and coherence, that it stops abruptly and inconclusively instead of coming to a satisfactory resolution and that it provides no "solutions" for the problems it depicts. Putting aside as beyond settlement, the question of whether an artist need "solve" problems that engage him, I would like simply to point out that in an earlier study of Steinbeck's fiction I try to demonstrate that *The Grapes of Wrath* is not a collection of disjointed episodes but a carefully worked out story that depicts the conversion of the Joads from a violent, self-centered family concerned only with preserving and perpetuating the clan, to a group of individuals who have learned from their own bitter experiences that man's survival depends upon the suppression of selfish instincts and the recognition of the dignity of every individual. As I have previously argued, the tableau at the end of the story in which Rosasharn Joad offers her breast to a dying stranger, "marks the end of the story Steinbeck had to tell about the Joads. Their education is completed. They have triumphed over familial prejudices. What happens to them now depends upon the ability of the rest of society to learn the same lesson they have already learned." [1]

As far as the central narrative about the education of the Joads is concerned, *The Grapes of Wrath* is not even truly what I have defined as a social novel. It stresses the achievement of individualism as much as the works of Thomas Wolfe and depicts the necessity of each individual's educating and reforming himself, rather than the causes of a national disaster. If the Joads had not been caught up in the events of a particular time and place that had profoundly affected Steinbeck and troubled his public, we might more easily recognize that their story belongs with Shakespeare's *The Tempest* and other masterpieces of the travail and triumph of the human spirit.

*The Grapes of Wrath* is, however, deeply rooted in depression-ridden America. It not only depicts some of the most harrowing events of the period, but it is also the outstanding artistic embodiment of a point of view that paradoxically both preserved the United States and held back its progress during the economic crisis. Steinbeck's novel is more closely related to Faulkner's *The Hamlet* than one might casually suppose. Both not only deal with conditions that blighted the nation, but also reflect similar viewpoints toward the causes and cure of that blight.

It is not really true that Steinbeck proposes no solutions for the problems that he depicts. Artist rather than social theorist, he implies rather than spells out his prescriptions; and some of the best-intentioned social reformers appear to lack the subtle gift for deciphering metaphors. The hints that he gives, however, show that his novel, far from representing an unusual or distinctive point of view, rests upon the same basic assumptions (the term *philosophy* seems inapplicable to any such unsystematic thinking) as a substantial body of work produced by some conservative intellectuals of the era.

*Conservative* may seem a strange word to apply to the author of *The Grapes of Wrath*, which many truculent defenders of the shabby *status quo* denounced as radical when it was published. Yet even though the novel was enthusiastically received in Russia as evidence of American decadence, relations between Steinbeck and the pro-Communist intellectuals of the thirties had been strained since the publication in 1936 of *In Dubious Battle*, at the end of which Steinbeck had metaphorically accused Red agitators of what he—like Hawthorne—considered the unpardonable sin—the exploitation and destruction of human beings for the advancement of an abstract cause. Before his disappearance, Doc Burton, the most sympathetic character in the novel, explains to the principal representative of the Party: "There've been communes before, and there will be again. But you people have an idea that if you can *establish* the thing, the job'll be done.

Nothing stops, Mac. If you were able to put an idea into effect tomorrow, it would start changing right away. Establish a commune, and the same gradual flux will continue." Asked if he doesn't think "the cause" is good, he replies, "I want to see the whole picture—as nearly as I can. I don't want to put on the blinders of 'good' and 'bad,' and limit my vision." [2]

Throughout his work, Steinbeck has always maintained that consideration for the individual human being must be placed above any cause or party. From *The Pastures of Heaven* to *Cannery Row*, he stresses constantly the essential loneliness of the individual and the necessity of the individual's accepting the often unpleasant responsibility for his actions and decisions. Even if he is destroyed, like Danny in *Tortilla Flat*, it is better that he die a free agent than live the captive of any system. Conservative ideas about the individual and his relationship to government have been quite conspicuous in Steinbeck's recent works like *Sweet Thursday* and *The Short Reign of Pippin IV*, but this conservatism marks no abrupt shift in his thinking. Steinbeck, who has always been preoccupied with the relationship between the individual and the group, indicated in such early stories as "The Raid" and "The Vigilante" that he disapproved of what happened if the individual submerged himself in the group.

Those who found symptoms of Leftist thinking in *The Grapes of Wrath* must have accepted one of Steinbeck's character's sarcastic description of a Communist as "any son-of-a-bitch that wants thirty cents an hour when we're payin' twenty-five" (p. 407).[3] There are only two passages—both in interchapters—that could be mistaken for radical propaganda.

> If you who own the things people must have could understand this, you might preserve yourself. If you could separate causes from results, if you could know that Paine, Marx, Jefferson, Lenin, were results, not causes, you might

survive. But that you cannot know. For the quality of owning freezes you forever into "I," and cuts you off forever from the "we." (p. 206)

And the great owners, who must lose their land in an upheaval, the great owners with access to history, with eyes to read history and to know the great fact: when property accumulates in too few hands it is taken away. And that companion fact: when a majority of the people are hungry and cold they will take by force what they need. (p. 324)

Read carefully in context, however, neither passage advocates revolt nor gives the author's view of what *should* happen. In both he speaks as an observer, warning what *may* happen—what it *regrettably* appears *will* happen. These passages, like the novel as a whole, are not rabble-rousing speeches inciting an outraged proletariat to rise against its oppressors; rather they are warnings to a comfortable and negligent propertied class to awaken it to what is happening around it. *The Grapes of Wrath* in its treatment of contemporary events is a cautionary tale.

Steinbeck does in the fifth chapter of the novel denounce the impersonal and irresponsible course that American business has taken through the twenties and thirties, and he depicts sympathetically those who rail at the "ridiculousness of the industrial life" (p. 385). But critics have not been sufficiently cautious in avoiding the fallacy of the undistributed middle when categorizing Steinbeck. Far from joining ranks with the "proletarian" authors of the thirties who rallied enthusiastically to the Communist cause, Steinbeck served as a spokesman of a "third force."

This group held, in the words of Herbert Agar, whose collaborators on *Who Owns America?* (1936) have exhibited little appreciation of Steinbeck, that the American dream of the independence of the individual was being "derided" by two groups—"the communists, who say that any attempt to realize it must be vain, since the attempt would contradict the laws of Marx; second, by the friends of Big Business, who dishonor the dream by saying that it has been realized, that it lies all about us today." [4] The contributors to *Who Owns America?* sought an alternative to both communism and Big Business that would free the capitalist system from the stranglehold of monopoly. Their search, like Steinbeck's, led to the idealization of the independent yeoman.

This important aspect of Steinbeck's thought has been recognized by only two previous critics of *The Grapes of Wrath*. Joseph Fontenrose observes that Steinbeck's " 'agrarian socialism' is really Chestertonian Distributivism, a society of small-scale farmers working their own plots," [5] and Chester Eisinger in the best analysis of the ideological underpinnings of the novel, "Jeffersonian Agrarianism in *The Grapes of Wrath*" argues that while a discussion of Jefferson's views "does not pretend to serve as an interpretation of the entire novel," it is closely associated "with what was apparently one of the primary motives for writing the book, the desire to protest against the harsh inequities of the financial-industrial system that had brought chaos to America in the thirties." [6]

Against Fontenrose's undeveloped assertion, it can be argued that while the parallel is basically sound, it is grossly oversimplified since Steinbeck and Chesterton operated from vastly different premises. Eisinger's cogent argument demands close scrutiny, but it does not suggest the extent of the effort in the thirties to win converts to an "alternative" to monopoly capitalism or communism that is too much limited when it is labeled simply "Jeffersonian."

Eisinger points out that the belief basic to Jefferson's doctrine is that "landed property held in freehold must be available to everyone" and that the independent farmer "acted in accordance with his own instincts or desires and rose or fell by virtue of his own efforts." It shared the primitivistic doctrine that "close contact with nature and with God makes and keeps men pure," whereas "the city is a cesspool of evil." [7] Steinbeck, Eisinger maintains, accepts and projects through his novel the notion that "the farmer draws spiritual strength as well as sustenance from the soil." [8]

In the fifth chapter that holds the key to the book's ideology, Steinbeck does have one of his anonymous migrants express what can only be described as the concept of a mystical union between a man and his soil.

> "Funny thing how it is. If a man owns a little property, that property is him, it's part of him, and it's like him. If he owns property only so he can walk on it and handle it and be sad when it isn't doing well, and feel fine when the rain falls on it, that property is him, and some way he's bigger because he owns it. Even if he isn't successful he's big with his property. That is so." (p. 50)

The real evil of corporate farming, Steinbeck clearly suggests, in a description of the driver of a tractor that is plowing up the tenants' farms for the remote and untouchable city corporation, is that it destroys this mystical bond between man and land.

> The man sitting in the iron seat did not look like a man; gloved, goggled, rubber dust mask over nose and mouth, he was a part of the monster, a robot in the seat.
>
> .   .   .   .   .   .   .   .   .   .   .   .   .
>
> He loved the land no more than the bank loved the land. . . . The driver sat in his iron seat and he was proud of the straight lines he did not will, proud of the tractor he did not own or love, proud of the power he could not control. And when that crop grew, and was harvested, no man had crumbled a hot clod in his fingers and let the earth sift past his fingertips. . . . The land bore under iron, and under iron gradually died; for it was not loved or hated, it had no prayers or curses. (pp. 48–49)

The blight of the corporate society as Steinbeck sees it is the same that Warren Beck points out Flem Snopes brought upon the Mississippi of Faulkner's *The Hamlet*—automatism. The city and the machine have broken the bond between man and the soil and have reduced man to a robot. Hence Steinbeck does not have his dispossessed farmers seek refuge in the city to which many had turned during agricultural depressions; rather they abandon their exhausted Midwestern soil in the hopes of claiming a new homestead in California where Ma Joad dreams that they "can get one of them little white houses" and "the little fellas go out an' pick oranges right off the tree" (p. 124). Both Faulkner's and Steinbeck's novels associate with the move from farm to city, the tragic havoc wrought by those who seek financial success rather than love.

Chester Eisinger notes in passing that the period of *The Grapes of Wrath* "saw also the growth of the back-to-the-farm movement and the proliferation of books guaranteeing independence, and even security, on five acres," [9] but writing at a time when many of the proponents of this back-to-the-soil movement were still vocal, he did not consider it necessary to linger over their tracts. *The Grapes of Wrath* has, however, because it is more than a single-minded tract, outlived the movement that it in part reflected. Today's readers are likely to regard Steinbeck as an isolated voice, and only by recalling some of the now largely forgotten expressions of similar sentiments can we understand his novel as a reflection of important patterns of social and economic thinking in the thirties.

## ii

The basic notion of the virtue of rural life long antedated Jefferson's eighteenth century. Paul H. Johnstone, tracing the history of "the praise of husbandry," finds its literary origins (its actual origins must be lost in antiquity) in the writings of Hesiod, Xenophon, and Cato, the last of whom in what is considered the oldest extant prose work in Latin, declared farmers better citizens than city dwellers.[10] This philosophy enjoyed a great vogue among the writers of Rome's Augustan Age; and, although it lost its appeal during the Middle Ages, when most men were grubbing out dreary existences on farms, it was revived by those Renaissance writers who showed an enthusiasm for all things Classic. After flourishing in the sixteenth century, the notion of rural virtue declined in the seventeenth, but revived vigorously in the eighteenth, reaching its climax during the reign of George I. The principal propagators of the doctrine in England were Richard Bradley, Stephen Switzer, and John Lawrence, who in *Paradice Regain'd* (1728) "illustrated the moral that gardening was the key to the recovery of terrestrial happiness." Although as the century progressed, Johnstone continues, "State favor was concentrated upon urban industry and commerce rather than upon agriculture, and . . . country life and residence was generally considered a misfortune to be avoided whenever possible," rearoused enthusiasm was reflected in works like Goldsmith's "The Deserted Village" and Thomson's "The Seasons" and principally in the writings of Arthur Young.[11]

Meanwhile in France a group called the Physiocrats were trying to organize one of the pioneering efforts at economic theory around the passion for rural life. Although an English banker, Cantillon, and a French court doctor, Quesnay, are often given credit, respectively, for formulating and systematizing the physiocratic concepts, the man principally responsible for their enthusiastic reception in the late eighteenth century was Victor de Riqueti, Marquis de Mirabeau, stern parent of the outstanding orator of the French revolutionary movement. Presenting quite a different face to his reading public than he showed his family, Mirabeau began publishing in 1758 a commentary on Cantillon, *L'ami des hommes*, which advanced the notion that "the small cultivator was to be encouraged and held in honour; the idle consumer viewed with reprobation," ideas which Eisinger points out are specifically illustrated by Steinbeck in his depiction of poor and rich travelers. Mirabeau also held that "an unequal distribution of wealth is prejudicial to production, for the very rich are 'like pikes in a pond' who devour their smaller neighbours." [12] Mirabeau argued that the great landowners should live on their estates and stimulate their development and that a ministry of agriculture should be created to bring to farming "the succour of applied science." That Mirabeau, through his impassioned writing, was the principal propagator of physiocratic doctrines, is evidenced by the honors that he received from dignitaries like the King of Sweden and from his becoming known himself as "the friend of man." Yet, although physiocratic theories were carried into practice in three villages in Baden, Adam Smith was not unduly cynical when he said that the notions had never been tried out. Nor was there much emulation of the example offered in *The Rural Socrates*, by Hans Caspar Hirzel, of Kliyogg Gouyer of Wermetschweil, Switzerland, who exemplified everything that Xenophon had said Socrates commended in men distinguished for "prudence and understanding." The French translation of Hirzel's book was, however, enthusiastically recommended by Mirabeau, and the English translation was sponsored by Arthur Young.

Even though Jefferson became a friend of Pierre Samuel du Pont de Nemours, one of the principal disciples of the physiocrats and, ironically, father of the founder of one of America's largest corporations, Gilbert Chinard, who edited the men's correspondence does not think that Jefferson was influenced by the French doctrines, but rather hit upon them independently.

Jefferson's most explicit statement about rural virtue is the earliest of his preserved references to the subject. In his *Notes on Virginia*, he wrote:

> Those who labor in the earth are the chosen people of God, if ever he had a chosen people, whose breasts he has made his peculiar deposit for substantial and genuine

virtue. . . . While we have land to labour then, let us never wish to see our citizens occupied at a work-bench, or twirling a distaff. . . . The mobs of great cities add just so much to the support of pure government, as sores do to the strength of the human body.[13]

Several years later he wrote in the same strain to John Jay from Paris.

Cultivators of the earth are the most valuable citizens. They are the most vigorous, the most independent, and the most virtuous. . . . As long therefore as they can find employment in this line, I would not convert them into mariners, artisans, or anything else. . . . I consider the class of artificers as panders of vice and the instruments by which the liberties in a country are generally overturned.[14]

Two years later, in 1787, in a letter to John Blair, he called "the pursuits of Agriculture, the surest road to affluence and best preservative of morals," and the next day he wrote to Washington, "The wealth acquired by speculation and plunder is fugacious in it's nature and fills society with the spirit of gambling. The moderate and sure income of husbandry begets improvement, quiet life, and orderly conduct both public and private." [15]

On such statements, what Eisinger calls the Jeffersonian myth has been erected, but Jefferson himself did not cling unalterably to these sentiments. Home from what must have seemed a depraved Paris and close to the soil once more, he showed that he had doubts even before the close of the eighteenth century about ideas that his followers still advocated in the twentieth. To Horatio Gates on February 21, 1798, Jefferson wrote, "How far it may lessen our happiness to be rendered merely agricultural, how far that state is more friendly to the principles of virtue & liberty, are questions yet to be solved." [16] By 1817 he was even less enthusiastic. To William Sampson he wrote:

I was once a doubter whether the labor of the Cultivator, aided by the creative powers of the earth itself, would not produce more value than that of the manufacturer, alone and unassisted by the dead subject on which he acted? . . . But the inventions of latter times, by labor-saving machines, do as much now for the manufacturer, as the earth for the cultivator. Experience too has proved that mine was but half the question. The other half is whether Dollars & cents are to be weighed in the scale against real independence? [17]

By the end of his life, however, Jefferson recognized that even the "real independence" of the agrarian life might be illusory. In a pathetic last letter to Madison written February 17, 1826, only a few months before his death, Jefferson, fearing that he might lose his beloved Monticello, observed:

the long succession of years of stunted crops, of reduced prices, the general prostration of the farming business, under levies for the support of manufactures & c., with the calamitous fluctuations of value in our paper medium, have kept agriculture in a state of abject depression which has peopled the Western States by silently breaking up those in the Atlantic and glutted the land market, while it drew off its bidders. In such a state of things, property has lost its character of being a resource for debts.[18]

Although he placed the blame for the calamitous agricultural situation upon the growth of industry, Jefferson recognized that however virtuous the life close to the soil might be, it was not in itself capable of preserving the individual's independence and integrity.

Jefferson's defection did not, however, deal the death blow to the ideas that he had earlier espoused. A similar view of the virtues of the agrarian life was advanced late in the nineteenth century by Pope Leo XIII, whose encyclicals have been called "the most important single contribution to catholic doctrine since the Middle Ages." [19] This first modern pontiff of the Roman Catholic church not to be burdened with the temporal administration of the Papal States, which Italy had absorbed in 1870, laid down the tenets of a new agrarianism in one of his most influential social encyclicals, *Rerum Novarum* (*Of New Things*), a statement about the condition of the working classes that vigorously attacks the increasingly influential doctrines of socialism.

Pope Leo thought that the appeals of this pernicious new movement might be countered by greater "distributive justice." He especially remarked that "the law . . . should favor ownership, and its policy should be to induce as many as possible of the humble class to become owners," since "if working people can be encouraged to look forward to obtaining a share in the land, the consequence will be that the gulf between vast wealth and sheer poverty will be bridged over and the respective classes brought nearer one another." He also argued that the policy would slow down migration, because "no one would exchange his country for a foreign land if his own afforded him the means of living a decent and happy life." [20]

There is no more reason to argue that Steinbeck was influenced by the *Rerum Novarum* than by physiocratic pronouncements, but it is interesting to note that when in the last of his newspaper accounts of conditions in the migrant camps, Steinbeck makes his only specific suggestions of immediate remedies for the situation, they parallel statements in the encyclical. Steinbeck's suggestions boil down to two: that labor unions regulate the use of migratory labor in agriculture and that the practice of encouraging an oversupply of labor in order to reduce wages be stopped.[21] Pope Leo had specifically observed that "the organization of workingman's associations be permitted and encouraged for helping each individual member to better his condition to the utmost in body, mind and property" and that "the rich must religiously refrain from cutting down workmen's earnings, whether by force, by fraud, or usurious dealings." [22]

If Pope Leo did not directly influence Steinbeck, he certainly did directly influence the "distributist" schemes of the "Chesterbelloc" as the neo-orthodox Britons G. K. Chesterton and Hilaire Belloc came to be collectively known. Under Belloc's influence, Chesterton became one of the principal propagandists for a "back-to-the-soil" movement in the twenties. The statement of Chesterton's distributist views in *The Outline of Sanity* (1927) proves to be little more than a verbiose and foggy statement of the ideas about the encouragement of small property holding expressed in the *Rerum Novarum*.

The practical program of the Distributists is hard to specify, for, as Maisie Ward, Chesterton's biographer, admits, "A most difficult question to answer is the degree of the League's success. Its stated aim was propaganda, the spreading of ideas." [23] Clearly the group favored "back to the soil" concepts calling for the creation of a large peasantry that would own its farms. In *The Outline of Sanity*, Chesterton argued:

> The primary case for the peasant is of a stark and almost savage simplicity. A man in England might live on the land, if he did not have rent to pay to the landlord and wages to pay to the labourer. He would therefore be better off, even on a small scale, if he were his own landlord and his own labourer.[24]

He proposed no specific laws or programs for making the peasant his own landlord and laborer, however. The most definite proposal in the book merely calls for a poll.

> We want to find out how many peasants there are, actual or potential, who would take over the responsibility of small farms, for the sake of self-sufficiency, of real property, and of saving England in a desperate hour. We want to know how many landlords there are who would now give or sell cheaply their land to be cut up into a number of such farms.[25]

The execution of some land redistribution program would

he felt be beneficial because "It is that satisfaction of the creative instinct in the individual that makes the peasantry as a whole content and therefore conservative." [26]

Thus far, as Joseph Fontenrose suggests, Steinbeck's arguments in *The Grapes of Wrath* parallel Chesterton's vaguely formulated scheme; when we consider, however, the fundamental assumptions underlying their concepts of land redistribution, the unbridgeable gap between them becomes apparent. Steinbeck would surely be chilled by Chesterton's quaintly affected use of the condescending term "peasant," and he would surely reject Chesterton's concept, as expressed in a chapter on "The Religion of Small Property," of the aim not just of distributism, but of all human endeavor.

> The time has come in every department, but especially in our department, to make once again vivid and solid the aim of political progress or colonial adventure. Even if we picture the goal of the pilgrimage as a sort of peasant paradise, it will be far more practical than setting out on a pilgrimage which has no goal. But it is yet more practical to insist that we do *not* want to insist only on what are called the qualities of a pioneer; that we do not want to describe merely the virtues that achieve adventures. We want men to think, not merely of a place which they would be interested to find, but of a place where they would be contented to stay. Those who wish merely to arouse again the social hopes of the nineteenth century must offer not an endless hope, but the hope of an end. Those who wish to continue the building of the old colonial idea must leave off telling us that the Church of Empire is founded entirely on the rolling stone. For it is a sin against the reason to tell men that to travel hopefully is better than to arrive; and when once they believe it, they travel hopefully no longer.[27]

As his other traditionalist leanings also suggest, Chesterton yearned for a static order and looked, as did Pope Leo XIII, to an economy based upon small independent farmers as the source of political and social stability.

Against this notion of the desirability of a fixed order must be placed Steinbeck's clearest statement of his own dynamic faith in *The Grapes of Wrath.*

> For man, unlike any other thing organic or inorganic in the universe, grows beyond his work, walks up the stairs of his concepts, emerges ahead of his accomplishments. This you may say of man—when theories change and crash, when schools, philosophies, when narrow dark alleys of thought, national, religious, economic, grow and disintegrate, man reaches, stumbles forward, painfully, mistakenly some- times. Having stepped forward, he may slip back, but only half a step, never the full step back. . . . If the step were not being taken, if the stumbling-forward ache were not alive, the bombs would not fall, the throats would not be cut. Fear the time when the bombs stop falling while the bombers live—for every bomb is proof that the spirit has not died. (pp. 204–5)

Steinbeck shares those "social hopes of the nineteenth century," expressed in Tennyson's and Browning's poems, that the reach must exceed the grasp, and the ideas of William Faulkner, who said in Japan:

> I don't hold to the idea of a return. That once the advancement stops then it dies. It's got to go forward and we have got to take along with us all the rubbish of our mistakes and our errors. We must cure them; we mustn't go back to a condition, an idyllic condition, in which the dream [made us think] we were happy, we were free of trouble and sin.[28]

The difference between the views represented, on the one hand, by Chesterton and, on the other, by Steinbeck and Faulkner are probably most admirably summed up in a passage from one of Jefferson's letters to Du Pont de Nemours that has been called one of the "great ideas" of Western man: "We both consider the people as our children, and love them with parental affection. But you love them as infants whom you are afraid to trust without nurses; and I as adults whom I freely leave to self-government." [29] In the most propagandistic part of *The Grapes of Wrath*—the description of the government camp—Steinbeck never implies that the government should take the responsibility for managing the lives of the migrants. He shows it only providing them with an opportunity to govern themselves. When Ma Joad asks the camp manager if he is the boss, he replies, "The people here worked me out of a job" and then explains how they have achieved the Jeffersonian ideal (p. 415).

A distinction must thus be made between the kinds of mystical agrarianism that Steinbeck advocates in *The Grapes of Wrath* and the twentieth-century calls Chestertonian, and those of a group of Southerners in *I'll Take My Stand* for a return to a patriarchal system that is assumed to have provided stability at some time in the vanished past. Steinbeck's novel is not a contribution to the literature of social regression, but to the literature of individual self-realization. Its traditionalism lies only in the author's clinging to what Eisinger considers the anachronistic notion that the best hope for man's self-realization lies in an intimate relationship with his own small plot of land and in an avoidance of the city that American writers and thinkers have so often denounced. In clinging to this idea Steinbeck was not alone. The myth of rural virtue dies hard in the United States.

### iii

This brand of mystical agrarianism did not arise, however, only in response to the unusual conditions of the depression; it had never disappeared from this country after Jefferson's time. The Homestead Act was especially an attempt to implement the back-to-the-soilers' dream of a state based upon independent freeholders. Most projects of the nineteenth century, however, were not—except in that they ultimately generally failed—of the same kind as those that have been advocated since the turn of the century, when the thinking culminating in expressions like *The Grapes of Wrath* began to develop after the frontier had vanished.

Many of the nineteenth-century projects, like the famed Brook Farm experiment, the Oneida community, the Fourierist groups, the Shaker colonies, the Amana communities in Iowa, were organized around some specific religious or political precepts and stressed not so much the independence of the individual as the advancement of the "cause." Many of them were basically communalistic. Some attempted to transplant vanishing cultures like "Merrie England's" to the Tennessee hills (Rugby) or the Kansas plains (Victoria). Second, a great majority of the clearly speculative projects were organized either by land companies or railroads to open up new territories and expand business. It would probably not have been possible for the modern variety of "back to the soil" enthusiasm to flourish while free lands remained and the nation was fundamentally agricultural, for too many persons would have been intimately acquainted with the unpleasant aspects of rural life to be taken in by a vision that emphasized only its imagined benefits. It was, as might have been expected, only when the chance to homestead was nearly gone that a nostalgic longing for lost opportunity began to manifest itself.

Certainly nineteenth-century American writers showed little response to the magic of the soil, except when an occasional Caroline Kirkland turned out a propaganda piece like *A New Home—Who'll Follow?* Emerson and Thoreau loved unspoiled Nature, but did not urge people back to the farm. Even Thoreau's *experiment* at Walden was, he stressed, exactly that; he did not intend to make subsistence farming a way of life. When late in the century fiction about the farm began to appear, the dismal picture painted by Mary E. Wilkins Freeman, Hamlin Garland, E. W. Howe, and Caroline Kirkland's son Joseph would scarcely have enticed readers to their own small plots. Even Frank Norris in *The Octopus*, although he defends the ranchers against the railroads, pictures the farmers themselves as speculators who do not love the land. The only character in the novel who is able to save himself, Vanamee, has to eschew civilization altogether, and back-to-the-soilers are not Rousseauists. Steinbeck shows his lack of interest in the recidivist who abandons organized society when he allows the Joad's oldest son Noah simply to wander down a river and out of the story altogether.

I do not intend to try to tell the whole involved story of the back-to-the-soil movement, but some of the highlights of the turn-of-the-century enthusiasm provide evidence of the assumptions behind the movement during the depression and of its chances of success.

The assumptions are perhaps most clearly stated in one of the earliest novels produced by the movement for which the novel provides the most appropriate name, *Back to the Soil* by Bradley Gilman. Published in 1901, the novel belongs to the same Utopian genre as Edward Bellamy's *Looking Backward* and William Dean Howells' *A Traveler from Altruria*, for Gilman sets forth his theories about the means of redeeming those long pent in city slums through his creation of an imaginary Circle City, within commuting distance of Boston. Gilman drew up an elaborate plan—complete with diagrams—for communities, that he felt would provide independence and stability at the same time by placing dwellings close together around a circular variation on the old village green and providing behind the houses, wedge-shaped holdings the sizes of which varied according to their intended use.

The most interesting passage in the fantasy occurs at the end, when the clergyman who has sponsored the venture meditates the sentiments that underlie it.

> Many a time, as I have watched our people going to their work or coming from it, talking interestedly on questions of

crops and fertilizers, and planting and harvesting, I have been reminded of the old myth of Antaeus, who was the son of Terra, the Earth; in wrestling with Hercules, he renewed his strength each time that he touched foot to the ground. That is the way with these colonists of ours; once pale, hopeless inmates of city alleys and cellars, now self-respecting, hopeful human beings, not perfect, not always appreciative of the help given them, but raised far above the vicious pauper level of their old life. They have gained strength, like Antaeus, by contact with Earth, the mother of us all, so far as our physical frames and senses are concerned. "The landless man has come to the manless land." Nature's balance is restored.[30]

The aphorism in the next-to-last sentence of the quotation is not original with Gilman, who produced besides this Utopian tale edifying children's books and religious tracts. The pithy sentiment was a favorite of Commander Frederick St. G. de Latour Booth-Tucker of the Salvation Army, son-in-law of founder William Booth and for a time head of American operations. In more expansive moments, Booth-Tucker worded the sentiment, "Place the waste labor on the waste land by means of waste capital, and thereby convert this trinity of modern waste into a trinity of production." [31] Under his aegis the Army embarked, beginning in 1890 in England, upon its only venture in farm colonization. When Booth-Tucker was sent to the United States in the late nineties, he made the formation of colonies his principal project. The first was begun at Fort Romie, California, on 520 acres in the Salinas Valley near Soledad. Unfortunately none of the eighteen pioneer families drawn from the city jobless were able to stick out a prolonged drought, and in 1901 the colony had to be reorganized.

Meanwhile a second had been started at Fort Amity, Colorado, near the Kansas border, in April, 1898, by Chicago families without farming experience. A third was organized in Ohio. Although the colonies were still flourishing enough in 1905 when H. Rider Haggard toured this country to inspire the popular novelist to argue that a large-scale project of the same kind should be launched in England, they had begun to languish when Booth-Tucker left the United States in 1904. The Colorado colony failed in 1908 as a result of poor soil, and the Ohio tract proved too small to be operated economically. The historian of the Salvation Army acknowledges that "as an experiment to remove the surplus population of the city to the country," the plan failed. As its critics had principally objected, "The expense of the colonies was out of proportion to the number of persons benefited." [32]

The frustration of this venture proved no deterrent, however, to others whose hearts leaped up at the thought of making pallid city dwellers hearty tillers of the soil. The motivation and results of the back-to-the-soil enthusiasm is nowhere better illustrated than by the history of the "Little Landers' Land Colonies" in Steinbeck's native California.

The presiding genius of this movement was William E. Smythe, who envisioned settling groups of families from all walks of life on one-to-five-acre plots.

> It was the expectation of the founder that each of these small farms, carried on under conditions of cooperation in regard to various activities, such as purchasing and marketing, would provide a living for a family. It was thought that a colony operating under such a plan would develop almost immediately a solidarity of feeling, and a most satisfactory social life.[33]

The philosophy behind the movement—Mr. Smythe's "The Hope of the Little Lands"—was emblazoned on a plaque mounted in the clubhouse of the first of the colonies.

> "That individual independence shall be achieved by millions of men and women, walking in the sunshine without fear of want.
> "That in response to the loving labor of their hands, the

earth shall answer their prayer: 'Give us this day our daily bread.'

"That they and their children shall be proprietors rather than tenants, working not for others but for themselves.

"That theirs shall be the life of the open—the open sky and the open heart—fragrant with the breath of flowers, more fragrant with the spirit of fellowship which makes the good of one the concern of all, and raises the individual by raising the mass." [34]

Three colonies were planted, the first in 1908 on 550 acres at San Ysidro, near San Diego, two miles from the Mexican border. Colonists came from all over the country, but a succession of disasters resulted in failure by 1918; by 1925 only one of the original colonists remained. Undeterred, Smythe began another at Los Terrenitos, seventeen miles from Los Angeles, in 1913. In this venture he was associated with Marshall V. Hartranft, who was to emerge a quarter of a century later as one of the bitterest critics of *The Grapes of Wrath*, which he could not perceive advocated the same kind of small farm economy that he did. Although Smythe parceled out 1700 acres of poor land into holdings that were too small, this venture was in a sense saved when it became profitable to subdivide the farms for the Los Angeles suburb of Tujunga. The original agrarian colony had disappeared by 1917.

Even while the first two ventures were dying, Smythe promoted another colony in 1915 at Hayward Heath, south of Oakland. Again he chose poor land, and not a single family made its living from its holding. The colony was defunct by 1920, but Smythe, like most who act upon their feelings rather than rational analysis, was unaffected by the results of the ventures, for in 1919 he became associated with the Secretary of the Interior, Franklin K. Lane, in an elaborate plan to extend the reclamation movement to the entire United States by placing soldiers returning from World War I upon subsistence homesteads.[35]

The basic reason for the failure of the "Little Lander"

colonies is unsentimentally summarized by Henry Anderson in his comment about the first colony at San Ysidro, "It was becoming evident that making a living upon the colony holdings involved more hard labor than most of the colonists had ever before performed." [36] Yet despite the repeated collapse of such ventures, the advent of the depression saw a host of "back-to-the-land" schemes enthusiastically received by publishers and public.

The specific link between these depression projects and earlier ventures that had aimed to clear slum-dwellers from festering cities is provided not by Gilman or Smythe, but by Bolton Hall, an Irish Presbyterian, born in Armagh in 1854. As a child he was brought to America, where he graduated at twenty-one from Princeton. Fellow members of the New York City University Club must have had misgivings about this outspoken lawyer who became an advocate of Henry George's theory of the single tax, organized both the city Tax Reform League and the first Longshoreman's Union, and crusaded for the conversion of vacant city lots into garden plots for slum dwellers. Hall eventually also became the prime mover in the development of Berkeley Heights, a garden suburb on the Lackawanna railroad at the extreme southwestern corner of Union County, New Jersey.

Hall's suburban experiences made him an enthusiast of the back-to-the-soil movement, which he advocated in 1907 in *Three Acres and Liberty* and subsequent works. Reviewing the initial essay the progressive *Arena* declared that among Henry George enthusiasts, "No one is doing so much practical work along several urgent lines as Bolton Hall" and averred that "Mr. Hall shows that it is not necessary for a man to go to a remote quarter in order to enjoy freedom and a reasonably prosperous life if he determines to master intensive cultivation of the soil and is wise in selecting his three acres." [37] On this last point, the reviewer for *The Dial* found Hall somewhat vague in specifying suitable localities; [38] nevertheless, the book was sufficiently well regarded to be reprinted as late as 1918, when it served to inspire Ralph Borsodi, who was to become the guiding spirit of the back-to-the-soil movement in the thirties.

### iv

This energetic and excitable young economist was the son of a New York and Scranton publisher of inspirational books for national advertisers, who had also written the introduction for one of Bolton Hall's back-to-the-soil tracts. The young Borsodi had organized a single-tax ticket in New York in 1918 and had subsequently become an economic advisor to Macy's and other large firms. He had actually begun his private "back-to-the-soil" movement in 1920, long before the depression; but it took this calamity to win his schemes national attention.

He first evidenced his gift for "how-to-do-it" books with *The New Accounting: Bookkeeping without Books of Original Entry by the Use of a Natural System of Double Entry Bookkeeping,* of interest in this account only because of the author's early use in an unexpected context of the term *natural* that was to pervade all his utterances. He followed up this utilitarian textbook with the privately published *National Advertising vs. Prosperity* (1923), part of his long warfare against what he considered one of the most insidious products of the machine age. He first attracted attention as a critic, however, in 1927 with the awkwardly titled *The Distribution Age: A Study of the Economy of Modern Distribution,* a continuation of his previous attack upon high-pressure advertising and installment-plan buying, much of which reads like an early version of Vance Packard's *The Hidden Persuaders.* The similarity between Borsodi's thinking and Steinbeck's while writing *The Grapes of Wrath* is apparent in this book, which opens with the charge that "every part of our economic structure is being strained by the strenuous effort to *market profitably what modern industry can produce,*" [39] a foreshadowing of Steinbeck's calling it, in the angry twenty-fifth chapter of *The Grapes of Wrath*, "a crime . . . that goes beyond denunciation," "a sorrow . . . that weeping cannot symbolize," "a failure . . . that topples all our success," the fact that "men who have created new fruits in the world cannot create a system whereby their fruits may be eaten" (pp. 476–77). Both Borsodi and Steinbeck agree that the fault lies in the system of distribution; but *The Distribution Age* hints only in a footnote at the back-to-the-soil thinking that would dominate Borsodi's later work: "The question of the responsibility for the high cost of distribution which may be attributable to our present system of land tenure would justify a volume exclusively devoted to that question." [40]

Two years later, only a few months before the stock market crash of 1929 that began the great depression, Borsodi in a long, expansive, "philosophical" work, *This Ugly Civilization*, applied the charges that he had previously made against high-pressure selling to the factory system as a whole. He maintained that the civilization that this system had produced was noisy, dirty, and "above all . . . ugly because of the subtle hypocrisy with which it persuades the people to engage in the factory production of creature comforts while imposing conditions which destroy their capacity for enjoying them." [41] The book is highly repetitive jeremiad, much of which is devoted— years before David Riesman—to explaining and illustrating the three classes of men—herd-minded, quantity-minded, and quality-minded. Borsodi's arguments are vulnerable on many points; but our interest is not in challenging him, but in determining what he contributes to an understanding of the back-to-the-soil movement. What had been implicit in the previous book becomes explicit in this one—that Borsodi's distaste for the factory system stemmed at least in part from a dislike of collectivism and a profound fear of automatism. He points out specifically the dehumanizing effects of a factory system "which has changed mankind from a race of participators in life to a race of spectators of it." [42] Three of eight evil effects that he claims the factory has upon the worker stress this charge: "It relentlessly mechanizes the workman and reduces all workers, except the few 'blessed' with administrative genius, to mere cogs in a gigantic industrial machine"; "It makes it almost impossible for individual workmen to be self-sufficient enough to develop their own personalities"; "It condemns not only the natural robot, but those capable of creative effort in the crafts, the arts and the professions, to repetitive work." [43] In one of his most extraordinary charges, he also claims that the factory system dehumanizes sex.

> As to the play aspect of our sex-life there can be no doubt that the factory is taking the place of the church as the greatest preventive of courtliness in sex-life. Against the church, Havelock Ellis and his disciples, notably Judge Ben B. Lindsey in the United States, may be winning; but against the factory they are almost certainly losing. The beauty which they are trying to infuse into sex-life by freeing us from the incubus of church dogmas is being withered by a factory-dominated civilization which turns us into irresponsible animals to whom sex means merely barbaric self-indulgence. [44]

Although *This Ugly Civilization* is full of suggestions of methods of home-baking, home-canning, and home-sewing, nowhere in it does Borsodi explain that he had gained his information on these subjects from his own family's experience. The impersonality of the work is surprising, since he had published in the *New Republic* in July, 1929, before the appearance of the book, three articles describing his way of life on an eighteen-acre homestead near New York City, which evoked several criticisms from scoffers. [45] Although Bruce Bliven had in an introductory article called Borsodi's experiment, "one of the most interesting" that he had heard of in many years, readers were not given a full account of it until the publication in 1933 of *Flight from the City*, inaugural book-length contribution to a genre that was to flourish for a dozen years as never before.

We can see in retrospect that the publication of this book was the high-water mark of Borsodi's career, although some of his later articles were more highly publicized. The account in the first seven chapters of this book of the Borsodis' agrarian venture is the most enjoyable of the writer's works, probably because he enjoyed sharing things that he had enjoyed doing. At the end of the seventh chapter, however, an ominous note of self-admiration is struck when Borsodi reflects that he hopes some day "a group of intelligent and cultured people may find it worth while to establish . . . a school of living." [46] Subsequently he was to found an institution with exactly this name, as one of the final steps in a career that illustrates the seemingly inevitable tragedy that ensues when a highly individualistic thinker tries to apply to society as a whole patterns that he has found personally satisfying.

The roots of this tragedy, which made Borsodi what Malcolm Cowley called "a dangerous messiah," [47] are to be found in the later pages of *Flight from the City*, which describe a scheme for the mass settlement of rural areas around Dayton, Ohio. Quoting near the end of the account of his own "homesteading" the Biblical story of Esau's sale of his birthright, Borsodi observes, "Surely it is plain that no man can afford to be dependent upon some other man for the bare necessities of life without running the risk of losing all that is most precious." [48] Yet in his account only a few pages later of the Dayton plan, he explains that an application has been made for federal assistance because "the local situation is such that without government aid the expansion of the homestead movement cannot proceed as rapidly as hoped for" and he also comments favorably on an arrangement that would prevent homesteaders from ever gaining title to their property (thus making them perpetually dependent on "some other man") "in order to prevent the possibility of speculation in land either at present or at some future time." [49]

Like most enthusiasts, Borsodi evidently failed to realize that both of these arrangements for expediting the realization of his vision would create the very dependency that he had denounced earlier in the book. Consistency is not the mark of the visionary, and Borsodi clearly believed that he had hit upon a panacea.

> Instead of spending more and more millions to support the unemployed while the depression is dragging its weary way over the years, why shouldn't we use the public's "will-to-give" to enable the unemployed to support themselves? Why shouldn't we furnish them land, tools, lumber, seed, livestock, wool, leather, raw materials of all kinds to enable them to establish themselves once again in the homesteads which they should never have abandoned as many of them did perhaps generations back? . . . If we did it on a sufficiently large scale, we would end the problem of unemployment for the whole country, and end it permanently. [50]

An uninfatuated observer might have been able to predict the next events. The sponsoring social agencies in Dayton actually received in 1933 the federal grant for which Borsodi had recommended they apply—not the two and a half million they had hoped for, but enough—$359,000. The next March, Secretary of the Interior Harold L. Ickes ordered the federalization of all projects receiving federal assistance. Embittered, Borsodi, who had quit his job in 1933 to devote all his energies to resettlement, denounced Ickes' action as a betrayal, withdrew as consulting economist of the project to embark upon a purely privately sponsored one of his own, and became more vehemently than ever a critic of government

activity, describing the FHA, for example, as "an install-
ment plan." [51]

Borsodi turned his attention to the long projected
School for Living, an agrarian colony founded in 1935 on
Haverstraw Road in Suffern, New York, under the direction of the Independence Foundation, which Borsodi
headed. By August four homesteads were underway and
similar colonies were projected in Somerset, Pennsylvania;
Richmond, Virginia; Elliot, Maryland, and the Adiron-
dacks. None of these materialized, but the original colony
had grown to nine houses with three more under construction when on October 17, 1937, the cornerstone was laid
for a Community Center to be built with funds raised by
Borsodi's lectures.

A careful observer of the venture might have felt misgiv-
ings about a note beginning to appear in these frequent
public lectures. In January, 1937, Borsodi had joined
Herbert Agar, an ally of the Southern agrarians, and
American enthusiasts of Chestertonian distributism, in the
publication of *Free America*, a monthly periodical that
Chesterton's biographer calls the most effective vehicle
anywhere for her subject's theories. Even earlier, in
October, 1936, Borsodi had begun to contribute to the
*American Review*, another agrarian organ that under the
editorship of Seward Collins became openly sympathetic
with the fascists. In his first contribution to this magazine,
which printed at least one article that argued that fascism
as practiced in Italy was "linked inseparably with the
soundest traditions of our civilization," [52] Borsodi presented the case for withholding absolute title from homesteaders in resettlement ventures. Looking over the possibilities for managing the projects, he unsurprisingly
rejected the government and argued that "the most desirable . . . would be the land co-operative in which the
actual leasing and development of the community was
entrusted to an adult educational institution of the type

being established at Suffern, New York." He did not feel obliged to explain that he headed this institution before sweeping on to his conclusion that such a plan "has the great ultimate advantage of experimenting with the Platonic ideal of a society directed by its teachers and philosophers." [53]

His other articles simply denounced federally subsidized slum clearance and announced that since people had lost "confidence in the power and integrity of the Federal government," the next depression—which was already on the way—would result in "a new leadership with a drastic and revolutionary program—either fascist or communist." [54] In a 1938 broadcast over New York City station WHN, he predicted even more dramatically that the adoption by the New York legislature of a public housing amendment would bankrupt the state, cause losses so great that home ownership would be abandoned, and simply create jobs for bureaucrats and fat profits for contractors.[55]

Despite Borsodi's increasing acerbity, the homestead project seemingly flourished; and despite his denunciations of government, he was called upon to collaborate with high officials of the Department of Agriculture in publishing in 1939 a book called *Agriculture in Modern Life*. Also in 1939 the Independence Foundation announced the launching of a new homestead project on the former estate of Mrs. Frances B. Still near Ossining, New York. Hardly more than a year later, a blow fell. Borsodi at last made the front page of the *New York Times*, but hardly in the manner that he must have dreamed he would. On Sunday, May 5, 1940, it was announced that he had resigned as president of the Independence Foundation and the associated projects and that he was entering a sanitarium for medical treatment.

The *Times* attributed the collapse of the venture to two causes: one was that "many of the homesteaders complain that Mr. Borsodi's zeal for overseeing details of the construction work, while at the same time concerning himself with theory in the School of Living, hampered rather than advanced the practical part of the program"; the other was that the homesteaders objected to the indentures that prevented their acquiring title to their lands. Two other deflating revelations were made. In the five years since its organization, the foundation had supervised the construction of only seventeen houses at the original site and an equal number at a second location in West Nyack. Only four homesteads had been started on Mrs. Still's former property, most of which would have to be disposed of, and only three had been established at a fourth project near Pompton Lakes, New Jersey, which the committee replacing Borsodi proposed to abandon. It was further disclosed that the movement had flourished to the extent that it had only because of the substantial funds invested by Chauncey D. Stillman, a New York architect. The *Times* writer provided the best possible summary for the complete story: "The whole scheme operated successfully in theory. In practice there was increasing resentment by some of the homesteaders over the Borsodi control of the practical side of the experiment." [56]

Thus only a month after the appearance of *The Grapes of Wrath* and scarcely a month before the Fall of Paris, the grandest scheme of one of the most starry-eyed advocates of the back-to-the-soil movement collapsed. Borsodi continued to operate the School of Living and magazines occasionally ran features about its activities, but its last widely publicized accomplishment was a dinner on September 15, 1943, at which Pearl Buck denounced any sort of postwar alliance between the United States and England and shuddered at the thought of the industrialization of China, Russia, and India, while Borsodi saw "catastrophic inflation" and "post-war depression." [57] He has since kept his books about decentralization in print and has published others, principally on education, which his experience has taught him the world needs before it is ready to appreciate his vision.

## v

Borsodi by no means had the field to himself during the thirties, although *Flight from the City* was the first book-length call to return to the soil. Curiously, nothing was heard of the movement during the first two years of the depression when the faltering Hoover administration tried to maintain the illusion that hard times weren't here to stay; even most of the accounts subsequently published dealt with efforts that started no earlier than 1932, when people began to overcome the paralysis induced by the evaporation of the seemingly endless boom.

That year the earliest magazine reports of new ventures appeared. Bellwether of the movement appears to have been a short, impassioned piece in *Forum* for July, 1932. The magazine had conducted a contest for "the most constructive essay" by a graduating college senior describing how he proposed "to meet the pressure of hard times." Winner was C. J. Thornquest, an English major from Miami University, Oxford, Ohio, who had expected to teach, but was instead "going back to the soil" to try to farm.[58] Nothing was heard of Thornquest's results, but *Forum* for March, 1933, carried Katrina Hincks's "A Home for $130: One Way of Beating the Depression," the story of two college graduates' experiences building their own cottage and farming in Connecticut. Still later the magazine published a similar account that Lucile Grebenc was subsequently to develop into a book. Meanwhile, in October, 1932, the *Saturday Evening Post* climbed on the new bandwagon by printing a series of letters in which Richard C. Brown, one of many victims of bank liquidations, recounted the first months of his efforts to find a new life on an eighteenth-century farm near West Chester, Pennsylvania.[59]

Thereafter periodical advisories become too frequent

even to enumerate in a hurried survey; books were slower
to appear, for publishers were as cautious as other business
men in the timorous thirties. Besides, one returning to the
soil would presumably have things to do besides write a
book. At last in 1935 Borsodi's account was supplemented
by Gove Hambidge's record in *Enchanted Acre: Adventures in Backyard Farming,* of his experiences in the 1920's
on what he chose to call a "sunstead" in New York's
Westchester County. Hambidge's rambling book, however, made no claims that his way of life would suit anyone
but himself; he had, in fact, serious reservations about
back-to-the-soil agitations.

No such reservations troubled Maurice G. Kains, whose
*Five Acres,* also 1935, with title expanded to *Five Acres
and Independence* in 1940, provided a slogan to rally
enthusiasts for the movement. Kains was no newcomer to
farming or propagandizing; he was nearly seventy and one
of the nation's most prolific agricultural writers. His publishing career had begun thirty-six years earlier with a book
on the cultivation of ginseng, and he had won friends
during the first World War as a leading advocate of home
gardening and canning. He was also to be heard from
during World War II as a proponent of victory gardening.
None of his other works, however, enjoyed the popularity
of *Five Acres,* which had already gone through sixteen
printings when Kains revised it in 1943. It was one of the
few books of this genre ever to be added to a popular
paperbacked series.

Although Kains specialized in detailed, practical advice,
he served, too, as philosophical keynoter for the movement. "Where," he asked, "can a boy or a girl acquire and
develop [the] qualifications [of a liberal education] so well
as on a farm, well managed by loving parents who are
enthusiastic business and domestic heads of the enterprise
and who explain and insist upon obedience to the laws of
nature as well as those of the land and who live in harmony
with their neighbors?" He had already answered the ques-

tion with a tribute to self-reliance explaining that "city existence is non-productive" and that the best thing about farm life is that it provides "the basis and superstructure of true success—development and revelation of character and citizenship in [one's] self, his wife, sons, and daughters." [60]

Other voices joined Kains's. In 1936 Dwight T. Farnham's *A Place in the Country* recounted the trials of turning ten acres near Westport, Connecticut, into a new home. Lucile Grebenc also told of her transformation of a rundown New England farm in *Under Green Apple Boughs*, and the first of a series of books imported from England to reinforce local accounts, Franklin Lushington's *Pigeon Hoo*, dealt with the conversion of an Elizabethan cottage into a modern homestead. *Who Owns America?*, which also appeared in 1936, devoted most of its pages to attacking large corporations and defending regionalism, but it found space for a newspaper account of what homesteader George Smith had accomplished in Arkansas and for Andrew Lytle's lyric reconstruction of a farmer's day.[61]

By January, 1937, when Ralph Borsodi joined Herbert Agar and others in launching *Free America*, those who had returned to the soil in the thirties had had both time and experience enough to collect their thoughts for now responsive publishers; but the peak of the movement came in 1938 when the governors of both Vermont and Wisconsin contributed chapters to Charles Morrow Wilson's *Country Living*, and a young novelist turned farmer won the back-to-the-soil movement recognition from both the *Reader's Digest* and the Book-of-the-Month Club with his autobiographical *R. F. D.*

Charles Allen Smart had already published two novels about the romantic problems of sophisticated Easterners at the end of the gaudy twenties, but they had attracted little notice. *R. F. D.* told of his move in 1934 to a century-old farm near Chillicothe, Ohio, where he became princi-

pally interested in sheep raising. The unusual success of
the book appears attributable to what *Time*'s reviewer
called its "boisterously Philistine" viewpoint. Smart was a
soil enthusiast with whom city intellectuals could achieve
rapport. He was a Harvard graduate; he wrote plays for an
attic theater in Chillicothe during his years down on the
farm, and he decorated his WPA outhouse with reproduc-
tions of Toulouse-Lautrec, Laurencin, and di Chirico.[62]

He was also one of the most beguiling pleaders for a
return to the soil. "Even the poorest and most ignorant of
them [farmers] probably get more fun out of their work,
itself, than most city workers get out of theirs," he advised.[63] Both Ralph Borsodi and John Steinbeck might
have seconded Smart's sentiment that the aim of life close
to the soil is not worldly gain: "My kind of farming is not
for incompetents and weaklings; it is for people who have
no interest in 'getting ahead,' who like animals and plants
more than machinery, processes more than figures, solitude
more than most company, and a hunting cap more than a
derby hat." [64] Despite this lyrical outburst and a novel,
*Rosscommon* (1944), about his concept of an agrarian
Utopia, Smart did not stay on the farm. He served in the
Navy in World War II and then returned to teaching;
ulcers obliged him to retire before he was fifty to San
Miguel de Allende, Mexico. After a few years' residence
there, he wrote a book commending its charms to others.

Smart found a major ally in 1938 in Henry Tetlow,
whose *We Farm for a Hobby and Make It Pay* was the first
of several about his return in 1932 to Medlock Farm, near
West Chester, Pennsylvania. Tetlow epitomizes the inability of back-to-the-soil enthusiasts to realize that their
private preferences may not be universally shared when he
comments, "It is impossible to contemplate my individual
experiment without speculating on the social and economic consequences implicit in the more general adoption
of such a way of life." He speculated that seven millions,

"a lot of people to move beyond the risk of sudden, catastrophic destitution," might be "repatriated" from the cities.[65]

After 1938 the flow of books subsided, and accounts of new pioneering in such familiar spots as Connecticut, Vermont, and Pennsylvania attracted little attention; readers began to demand reports from more exotic locales. The Right Reverend Msgr. Luigi G. Ligutti and the Rev. John C. Rane told in *Rural Roads to Security* (1940) of the Granger Homestead experiment among Iowa coal miners; Mrs. Eva Paisley (*Sanctuary*, 1940) and Mrs. Louise Dickinson Rich (*We Took to the Woods*, 1942) enjoyed some success with accounts of retreats to the Maine woods, and Marguerite Lyon proved one of the most prolific contributors to the genre with a series of books about her family's experience in the Ozarks: *Take to the Hills* (1941), *The Green Grass Grows All Around* (1942), and *Fresh from the Hills* (1945).

I have by no means attempted to compile an exhaustive list of back-to-the-soil writings, but only to demonstrate that such books abounded before and during the period of the great success of *The Grapes of Wrath*. Many literate Americans seemed to yearn for the same kind of white cottage that Ma Joad did, and few of them seemed to have bothered to qualify their dreams with the cautious "maybe" that Ma did when she thought about "how nice it's gonna be" (p. 124).

So plentiful did "back-to-the-soil" books become that few reviewers even noticed Walter M. Pratt's account in *Adventure in Vermont* (1944) of the restoration of yet one more colonial farmstead. To attract attention it became necessary to hit upon provocative titles like Milton Wend's *How to Live in the Country without Farming*, which—as one reviewer perceived—was "definitely not 'for every one who is country-minded,' " but "rather for those in what economists call the middle and upper income brackets—or for people who just like to dream about having a place in the country, but never actually do anything about getting it." [66]

Like many enthusiasms, the back-to-the-soil movement found in its waning days the spokesman who—perhaps with a desperate knowledge that public interest was flagging—most clearly articulated the philosophy underlying all the frantic activity. Strictly speaking, Elmer Peterson's *Forward to the Land* (1942) does not belong in this account, for it was designed to preach conservation rather than homesteading; nevertheless both the former editor of the popular home-making magazine *Better Homes and Gardens* and "Ding" Darling, the popular cartoonist who introduces the book, make statements that might have served as rallying cries if the movement could have been revivified. Darling observes that "anyone who 'lists to nature's teachings' must be impressed by the primitive and timeless wisdom of those who have lived long and thoughtfully, in harmony with the unalterable faith of nature." Peterson, who devotes most of his book to a contrast between "soilways" and "moneyways" that would have intrigued Ralph Borsodi, pays perhaps the supreme tribute to those who work the soil.

> American farmers, in general, can be trusted to think things through to a sound conclusion. They come from the soil. They are close to the soil. They reason out their problems on the basis of fundamental things. . . . It is a revealing experience to think between plow handles, or in the company of an intelligent horse.[67]

Curiously, the man whose name has been since the end of World War II most prominently associated with the back-to-the-soil movement joined it only after it had lost its hold on the public. Louis Bromfield has, however, always been out of step with the times. Back in the supposedly sophisticated twenties when "hayseeds" were the targets of satirists like Sinclair Lewis and Ring

Lardner, Bromfield produced a serious trilogy of novels about farm life—*The Green Bay Tree, Possession,* and *Early Autumn*—that caused critics to regard the author as one who might deal significantly in fiction with the social issues of the thirties. With the coming of the depression, however, Bromfield did an about face and after *The Farm* (1933), until the end of the war, published exclusively sensational potboiling romances, often about India and other remote strands. Indeed his contributions to literature during the period discussed in this book were *Night in Bombay* and *Wild is the River,* both tailored to provide some of Hollywood's most glamorous stars with titillating roles. Kunitz and Haycraft in *Twentieth Century Authors* report that Bromfield resented being expected to live up to the promise of his early novels.[68]

After the war, however, when the back-to-the-soil movement seemed exhausted, Bromfield embraced it; and in the very year (1945) that others were abandoning the championing of rural virtue, he wrote *Pleasant Valley* to harangue the public about the social implications of his own Malabar Farm in Ohio. Perhaps Bromfield's persistently swimming against the literary current simply exemplifies his extreme and unshakable individualism. The more he insisted on talking about his farm, however, the less the public seemed to care to listen.

The death-blow to public enthusiasm for the back-to-the-soil movement had been administered, also in 1945, by the publication of Betty MacDonald's *The Egg and I,* the rollicking account of a young bride's misadventures on a western Washington chicken ranch. Returning veterans who might have been seduced by agrarian appeals were caught instead by Mrs. MacDonald's sardonic inquiries: "Why in God's name does everyone want to go into the chicken business? Why has it become the common man's Holy Grail?" (p. 38).[69] Like others, she and her husband had felt the mystical lure of the land and had believed that they "should hurry and move in" to help a neglected little farm "in its fight against the wilderness" (p. 47), but where earlier writers professed to have found joy, Mrs. MacDonald found only disillusionment.

> I confess I could hardly wait for our chicks to come and spent many happy anticipatory hours checking the thermometer and reveling in the warmth and cleanliness of the new brooder house. But I learned to my sorrow that baby chickens are stupid; they smell; they have to be fed, watered and looked at, at least every three hours. Their sole idea in life is to jam themselves under the brooder and get killed; stuff their little boneheads so far into their drinking fountains they drown; drink cold water and die; get B. W. D.; coccidiosis or some other disease which means sudden death. The horrid little things pick out each other's eyes and peck each other's feet until they are bloody stumps. (pp. 134–35)

Even the home canning that was Ralph Borsodi's special delight left Mrs. MacDonald cold: "the canning season was on. How I dreaded it! . . . Frankly I don't like home-canned anything" (p. 177). Life became a succession of encounters with drunken Indians and irresponsible neighbors; marriage became "a halloo from the brooder house porch to the manure pile" (p. 106).

Anyone with a lingering longing for the life close to nature must have been put off when the MacDonalds' most grotesque and ludicrous experiences were emphasized in the motion picture version of *The Egg and I*, starring Claudette Colbert and Fred MacMurray, which reached a far wider audience than any of the books by farm enthusiasts. The principal achievement of this anti-rural travesty was to introduce to the screen the MacDonalds' degenerate borrowing neighbors, Pa and Ma Kettle, who in the persons of Marjorie Main and Percy Kilbride romped through a series of pictures that provided post-World War II America with what was probably the most influential stereotype of the American yeoman as comic lout. Small wonder that after a brief flurry of activity in 1948 the back-to-the-soil movement subsided. *Free America,* for a decade the standard bearer of the diehards, had ceased publication early in 1947.

### vi

Did the back-to-the-soil movement of the depression years accomplish anything? In practical terms, remarkably little; but it did reflect an important pattern of American thinking and provided in its literature the record of this thought. T. J. Woofter, Jr., and Ellen Winston point out in *Seven Lean Years* that between 1930 and 1935 the farms of less than twenty acres that the back-to-the-soilers advocated did increase by more than thirty-six per cent.[70] It is doubtful, however, that literary enthusiasts did much to encourage this movement, because the only year in which more people went back to the farm than left it was 1932, before even Ralph Borsodi launched the new wave of homesteading literature with his account of the Dayton Plan. Because of the inherent lag in getting books written and printed, most of the literature of the movement appeared after enthusiasm had subsided.

It is even more doubtful that the movement resulted in the benefits that its literary proponents claimed for it. As early as 1932 when the first enthusiasm for ending the depression by returning to the soil developed, L. C. Gray of the Federal Bureau of Agricultural Economics pointed out that the "record of experiments" with homestead colonies of unemployed persons "is not a happy one." [71] The authors of *Seven Lean Years* point out that "Farm increases from 1930 to 1935 were most pronounced in areas around cities and in part-time and subsistence farming areas"; yet:

large numbers of people on the relief rolls of the Appalachian-Ozark Area and the cut-over area around the Great Lakes were engaged in farming, although their usual occupations were nonagricultural. They had lost their jobs, tried farming, and failed to produce enough to keep off relief. Much of the back-to-the-farm movement during the depression was of this character.[72]

In the same year that Steinbeck told of the Joads' quest for a new farm home in fertile California, Woofter and Winston gloomily concluded:

> Since the overwhelming majority of [children today] are growing up in farm and village homes, it is evidently futile to expect great relief for the unemployed in the cities through a back-to-the-farm movement. An already burdened agriculture has no room for the farm increase and stability is to be expected not from a back-to-the-farm movement but from the opposite trend.[73]

More recently, editor and agricultural economist Lauren Soth has been even more outspoken in *Farm Trouble.*

> Speeding up the movement of some farmers out of agriculture would permit those who remain to increase the size of their operations and raise their incomes. . . . Such a homesteads-in-reverse program . . . would prevent a great deal of hardship.[74]

Experts thus advocate the very kind of large-scale impersonal farming that Steinbeck denounces. The wisest character in *The Grapes of Wrath* from the point of view of professional students of agriculture is Connie Rivers, who wishes to learn to repair radios and settle down in town. Steinbeck's viewpoint toward those who think of giving up their agricultural heritage is shown, however, by his painting Rivers in especially black colors as a depraved individual capable of committing the gravest social offense by abandoning his pregnant wife.

What concrete evidence can be assembled dashes the claims of back-to-the-soil enthusiasts. Probably the most ambitious and best organized effort during the depression to put man back in contact with nature, was the government-subsidized Greenbelt Plan that resulted in the building of three model communities in Maryland, Illinois, and Wisconsin. Although this experiment was widely hailed, its historian, Paul K. Conkin, is obliged to admit that "compared to many other New Deal experiments, this community project was relatively small in terms of final accomplishments." [75] The most valid criticism, he acknowledges, is that its cost is high. It did not provide the anticipated low cost housing, any more than the Salvation Army's experiment had decades earlier, and when the government finally liquidated its interest in the venture between 1949 and 1952, it was able to realize only about fifty-three per cent of the original costs.

The failure was not, however, just financial, as Conkin ruefully admits.

> The community idea, so appealing in the abstract, was much more difficult to achieve in actuality than almost anyone believed possible in 1933. . . . All too often the settlers were not anxious to participate in experimental reform leading to a new America which they could not understand or appreciate. They simply wanted economic security.[76]

Conkin puts his finger on precisely what most back-to-the-soil theorists learned regretfully: the idea is appealing in the abstract to intellectuals, but it has little appeal for the vast majority of the people whom the intellectuals hope it may reclaim, since these people are seeking the greatest possible economic security in return for the smallest possible investment of their time and effort. Paul H. Johnstone and Bernard R. Bell make this point inescapably in A Place on Earth (1942), a critical appraisal of the government's subsistence homestead program during the depression, when they report that the implication of their findings is that "for most people, subsistence homesteading with great emphasis upon subsistence production is not a preferred way of life and is not regarded as a permanent type of adjustment." [77]

They go on to say that, in the light of this first government-financed program, "We need to gauge more accurately the opinion of those for whom the program is designed rather than the opinions of those to whom it appeals essentially either as a moral or a sentimental step."[78] Earlier, Johnstone had maintained (in contradistinction to the assertions of the back-to-the-soil enthusiasts who abhorred large-scale farming and mechanization), that since the eighteenth century it had been increasingly possible "to retain proprietorship of the land only by candid recognition of the new commercial nature of society and complete adaptation of farming practices to meet new conditions."[79] In the light of such a statement, Chester Eisinger is fully justified in observing that "we cannot use and cannot achieve agrarianism as a formal way of life" in modern America and that "the bankruptcy of Jefferson's ideal is only too well illustrated in the fact that the family-size farm continues to disappear from the American scene."[80]

In thus reiterating the sentiments of professional students of agriculture in a discussion of *The Grapes of Wrath*, however, Eisinger does not really answer Steinbeck, because novelists write, as Faulkner has said, about people who behave as the novelists believe they should.[81] The literary back-to-the-soil movement was not a carefully reasoned effort to solve the problems of a depression-ridden society, but the expression of a nostalgic longing for an uncomplicated, individualistic society that may never have existed anywhere. Andrew Lytle, one of the staunchest and most gifted of the Southern agrarians, sums up the spirit behind the movement when he says that a farm "is a form of property . . . that the average man can understand, can enjoy, and *will defend*. Patriotism to such a man has a concrete basis."[82] Agrarianism is the enduring faith of those resentful and distrustful of abstractions that threaten to reduce men to automatons. While the shocking portrayal of contemporary events may have been responsible for the extraordinary interest in Steinbeck's novel, it is difficult not to believe that one reason for the enduring popularity of *The Grapes of Wrath* is its giving voice to one of its readers' most cherished sentiments, for novels, after all (to use the language of the government report), are read not by those for whom back-to-the-soil programs are designed, but by those to whom they appeal "essentially either as a moral or sentimental step." One of the major reasons that Americans resisted collectivist propaganda as strongly as they did during the depths of the depression is almost surely that the American dream was still based on the notion that the most virtuous society is composed of small, self-sufficient tillers of their own soil.

The unkindest cut of all, then, to the sharers of the Dream is another paragraph from Johnstone and Bell's *A Place on Earth*, summarizing the answer of those connected with government homestead projects to a question about the relationship of the enterprise to the dominant social trends and forces of the period.

> It may be pointed out, in conclusion, that no reply refers to one of the more elusive purposes of the subsistence-homesteads program, as that program was conceived in certain quarters—the recapture of the supposed virtues of attachment to the soil. Some of the supporters of the program believed that the return of industrial workers to the land would strip them of what they considered to be false and evil urban values and ways of living. A plot of earth and work with the soil, they hoped, would re-endow them with the many virtues considered to be peculiarly attached to living on the land. None of the observers report any such change in values or patterns of living.[83]

Forceful as it is as a picture of social problems that demanded attention, therefore, *The Grapes of Wrath* is also a monument to some of the insupportable basic assumptions of the isolationist, agrarian-oriented America that was in its death throes even at the time of the publication of this most popular fictional evocation of the Dream.

THE MAJOR DIFFERENCE between Ernest Hemingway's *For Whom the Bell Tolls* and the two novels so far considered is that the actual event with which Hemingway concerns himself was over when the book appeared. When *The Grapes of Wrath* was published, the California vigilantes were still pushing migrants around and when *The Hamlet* appeared the last and loudest of the "rednecks"—Bilbo and Representative John Rankin—still sullied Congress with their presence. But when Hemingway's novel was published the Spanish Civil War was history. Franco had announced on March 29, 1939, that resistance had collapsed. Hemingway was, therefore, not cautioning the world about a present evil. Even the title of his work was elegiac.

The funeral orator may adopt a variety of approaches. He may linger nostalgically and sentimentally over the real or imagined virtues of the deceased, as Margaret Mitchell did in the best-selling *Gone with the Wind.* He may vent his wrath on the malefactors who have destroyed goodness, as Kenneth Rexroth does in his elegy on Dylan Thomas or as Hemingway himself had in *A Farewell to Arms* long after the first World War. Or he may threaten his readers with a fate similar to the cadaver's, as Sinclair Lewis had in *It Can't Happen Here* following the destruction of democracy in Germany and Italy. Hemingway's longest and long-awaited novel, however, follows none of these familiar patterns. It simply relates, in the journalistic style that had become its author's trademark, the events of three days preceding the death of an American dynamiter who has been working behind enemy lines with Spanish Loyalist guerillas.

Rather than leaving the reader with a neatly articulated account of the disaster, the novel leaves him with three principal problems: Why does Hemingway stress as he does the brutalities of the side with which he and his protagonist were associated? Why does he choose to place the action in a small, isolated guerilla camp? Why does he manipulate the concluding events so that the American demolitions expert faces his death covering the retreat of the remnants of the guerilla band? To suggest answers to these questions, I must first consider the civil conflict in Spain and the writings of Hemingway during the decade that culminated in the publication of *For Whom the Bell Tolls*.

It is difficult for those who lived through the trying days to realize that a whole generation is unacquainted with the Spanish Civil War and the reasons for its provoking a singular reaction among Americans during the troubled thirties. The turmoil in Spain had actually begun with the decade when in 1931 King Alphonso XIII was overthrown and a Republic established. Because of contention between Rightist and Leftist parties, neither of which could consistently rally majority support, the Spanish Republic never achieved stability.

In the general elections of 1936 a Popular Front coalition of middle-class liberals and leftists won a tenuous majority in the Cortes, the Spanish parliament. On July 13, the rightist militarists, led by exiled General José Sanjurjo, rose against this government. The General, however, was killed in a plane crash during his flight back to Spain to assume command of the revolutionary force, and the mantle of leadership fell upon the willing shoulders of the young General Francisco Franco.

The rebels, starting from bases in the Canary Islands and Spanish Morocco, made rapid gains. They captured Toledo in September, 1936, and besieged Madrid itself in 1937. For almost three years, the Loyalists conducted a remarkable defense; but they were defeated at last because of the extensive support that Franco received from Germany and Italy, while the democratic nations refused to give active support to the Loyalists. Only Russia, seeking to expand the sphere of Communist influence, actively aided the Loyalists, and Russia was in no position to match the contributions of the Fascist nations to Franco's forces. Communist assistance appears, if anything, to have antagonized much of the rest of the world into maintaining its shortsighted policy of staunch neutrality. Spain passed, almost by default, into the hands of the totalitarians.

Still, the rising generation is likely to ask what was especially significant about this civil conflict in Spain. Henry Steele Commager provides in a few words an analysis that ponderous commentaries have not improved upon.

> Although the Republican régime was not a democratic one in the American sense, and although it failed conspicuously to maintain order and safeguard liberty and property, it was clear that its defeat would constitute a severe setback for democracy and signal triumph for the forces of reaction and lawlessness.[1]

Spain afforded the Fascist states with the opportunity to conduct live maneuvers preparatory to their own contemplated aggressions, and encouraged them to become constantly more daring by fostering their belief that the democracies were impotent and could not be roused into action in defense of their own interests.

This Spanish Civil War thus assumed an importance far beyond the boundaries of impoverished and anachronistic

Spain as the first great conflict between the rising forces of fascism and the seemingly decadent democracies. As Hemingway's American, Robert Jordan, says to himself as he waits death near the end of the novel, "If we win here we will win everywhere" (p. 467).[2] He clearly feared, however, that the opposite was true. Most of the world selfishly hoped, on the other hand, that the conflict might be contained within Spain and that by sacrificing this "expendable" power to the rapacious totalitarians, as Manchuria and Ethiopia had already been sacrificed, the conquerors might grow sated and spare the democratic heartland. Most of the world nourished itself desperately on the illusion that the menace of the Axis powers would prove to be but a bogeyman, while a handful like Hemingway and the volunteers for the Loyalist International Brigades argued that the bell that tolled for Spain, tolled also for the hopes of the Western world, if not indeed for that world itself.

Yet Hemingway's novel is not exactly what its title might lead one to expect. This meditation is directed, like John Donne's from which the title is borrowed, not to the leaders of the free world, but to the seemingly helpless individual—not to submerge himself in some cause or mass movement, but to act and if necessary die as an autonomous person. Those who wished for a rebel victory in Spain to satisfy their personal lust for power defamed the Loyalist cause by equating it with communism. Hemingway attempted to get behind the labels that oversimplified the world's concept of the struggle and to force the isolated individual to recognize his own demanding responsibilities.

Hemingway's enormous reputation in the thirties rested largely upon his fictional reaction to World War I, *A Farewell to Arms*, in which the hero, sick of slogans and hysteria, makes "a separate peace" and disassociates himself from the war in order to enjoy a brief period of happiness with his beloved, before ultimately being defeated by the vagaries of nature. Seemingly following the doctrine that his hero had enunciated, Hemingway had consistently refused to identify himself with any slogan-mongering parties or "causes" and had exhibited an apolitical absorption in such manly sports as big game hunting and bullfighting. His indifference to the economic and political crises of the thirties was distinctly not popular in intellectual circles, because during the depression commitment on the artist's part was fashionable. Hemingway, the idol of the disillusioned, found himself a pariah as socially conscious litterateurs who could not afford to remain in Paris during the depression returned home to America to proclaim the new millennium.

Hemingway's espousal of the Loyalist cause during the Spanish Civil War was hailed, therefore, as one of the great about-faces in literary history. As Leftist critics eventually learned to their disgust, however, it wasn't an about-face at all. Hemingway had never veered far from championing the kind of almost anarchical individualism that had led Frederic Henry in a A Farewell to Arms to make his "separate peace." Looking back on Hemingway's work during the thirties, we realize how desperately the literary evangelists of the period must have sought to read what they wished between the lines when they claimed Hemingway as a convert to a particular camp.

## ii

The strongest evidence of the basic consistency between Hemingway's position in 1929 when he published A Farewell to Arms and 1939, although he may have vacillated during the interim, is a short story, "Under the Ridge," which appeared shortly after the collapse of Republican Spain in Hearst's Cosmopolitan, one of the most popular organs of middle-class isolationism.

This uncollected tale has no plot, but consists simply of

grim vignettes of two soldiers that an American (much like Hemingway) making a film (much like his *The Spanish Earth*) encounters one day on the front lines, and of the story one of these men tells of another soldier. The principal character is an unnamed Spaniard who identifies himself only as from Extremadura, one of the country's proudest and most xenophobic provinces. Like his fellow provincials, this soldier hates all foreigners, and he has especially good cause. He hates the English because they killed his great-grandmother during the Peninsular Wars. He hates the North Americans because his father died a conscript in the Spanish-American War. He now hates the Russians, too, because of what they did to Paco.

Paco was a nervous youth who had shot himself in the hand rather than go into battle. After his hand is amputated and he recovers in the hospital, two Russian battle policemen bring him to the very spot where he inflicted his wound and there, without trial or warning, they shoot him in the head as a horrible example to others. The reporter tries pallidly to argue that an army must be disciplined, but the bitter Extremaduran replies, "And to live under that sort of discipline we should die?" [3]

The same two Russians that had the previous day killed Paco, reappear in pursuit of a middle-aged French "comrade" who has shortly before passed the Extremaduran and the American. The stalkers find their quarry and shoot him, to the further disgruntlement of the Spanish soldier and the distress of the film-maker. In the first description of this Frenchman, the author violates the deadpan style in which most of the story is told to write an unexpectedly emotional passage that suggests the strong similarity between this character and Frederic Henry of A *Farewell to Arms*.

> I understood how a man might suddenly, seeing clearly the stupidity of dying in an unsuccessful attack; or suddenly seeing it clearly, as you can see clearly and just before you

die; seeing its hopelessness, seeing its idiocy, seeing how it really was, simply get back and walk away from there as the Frenchman had done. He could walk out of it not from cowardice, but simply from seeing too clearly; knowing suddenly that he had to leave it; knowing there was no other thing to do.[4]

It is to this man that the author returns at the end of the story to comment that it is he, if anyone, who has enjoyed a victory that day. The manipulation of the situation makes it clear that Hemingway's sympathies in 1939 lay, as they had in 1929, with the man who has the strength to make "a separate peace," though this tale is even more bitter and disillusioned than A *Farewell to Arms*. Frederic Henry does escape the hysterical carbinieri to enjoy some brief days of happiness, but the relentlessly efficient Russians see that this Frenchman's victory lasts only minutes. It is difficult to imagine how a story could more directly indict the Communists as the destroyers of what the author thought most valuable in the world—inexperienced, willing youth and self-possessed maturity.

One further barb aimed at the Russians is of particular significance. Asked if the Communists are fighting in his home province, the Extremaduran replies, "There are no Russians in Extremadura, and there are no Extremadurans in Russia." [5] Later he suggests that, although he personally wishes the American no ill fortune, he thinks it is time that the other left not only the rest area but Spain itself. Foreigners, the Extremaduran repeatedly asserts, have no business even criticizing the conduct of the war. This man from one of Spain's most isolationist provinces has much in common with the provincial Americans from Hemingway's native Tribuneland, as Colonel McCormick christened the region served by his isolationist Chicago newspaper. Although the American comments that he is getting tired of the Extremaduran (as less single-minded people tired of the *Tribune*'s tirades), he does not satirize his xenophobia, and he ultimately respects his wishes. The story has the curious effect of suggesting a sympathy for isolationism by a man regarded as a potent and outspoken interventionist. Exactly what was Hemingway's position with regard to American participation in the Spanish conflict? If he did not believe that our nation should have come to the military support of the Loyalists, what was the point of his own efforts on their behalf? The answer appears to be that Hemingway defended as *individual* action what he denounced as *group* action and that he remained consistently as vigorous an opponent of governmental intervention as many of the principals of the back-to-the-soil movement discussed in the previous chapter.

The best way to follow Hemingway through the thirties is to peruse the slick pages of *Esquire*. It is hard today to believe that this almost senescentally respectable fashion magazine was once considered as daring and controversial as *Playboy* and the galaxy of ruttish imitators that have usurped *Esquire's* former place. Arnold Gingrich's brainchild was founded, like *Fortune*, during the depths of the depression as a gauntlet hurled in the face of the defeatism of the times. It was unconservative in format, price, and content. It offered the young bucks of the down-at-the-heels period a rakish elegance that appears almost unbelievably tasteless today and a stable of the biggest names of the period, who were mostly pathetically anxious for any kind of remunerative commission. To lead off the first issue and many others during the first two years, Gingrich cannily chose Hemingway, symbol of audacity and virility, who contributed a series of "letters" from Cuba, Spain, Paris, Tanganyika—all the exotic spots that his name had made legend to those whose own romantic wings the depression had clipped. The magazine was a more immediate and overwhelming success than its nervous sponsors had dared dream. With the second issue (January, 1934), it was converted from a proposed quarterly into a no-wit-less garish monthly, appearing more often than Hemingway was able to dash off suitable letters.

Most of Hemingway's correspondence to this flashy gazette simply confirmed what the world already knew about his sporting interests, but he could not resist occasionally dropping the reporter's mask and sounding off. Two excerpts from early letters are of particular interest in establishing his attitude toward American involvement in European imbroglios. From Madrid, Hemingway wrote back in the days of the shaky Republic:

> A good deal more money is coming in in taxes than the royal establishment ever received, but now that money goes to the innumerable functionaries of the republic. These spread all over the country and while the peasants are as bad off as ever, the middle class is being taxed more than ever, and the rich certainly will be wiped out, although there is no sign of it yet; a great new bureaucracy is having more money than it ever had before and going in for much comfort, many vacations and considerable style. Politics is still a lucrative profession and those in the factions on the outside promise to pay their debts as soon as they get their turn in power.[6]

This cynical reflection about the Republic that would soon come under attack shows that, whatever Hemingway's sympathies during the Civil War, he had no illusions about the Loyalist state as specially virtuous. He chose sides with eyes wide open from the beginning to the shortcomings of all parties.

Even more significant as an indicator of his viewpoint is one of the closing comments in his next letter, from Paris.

> What makes you feel bad is the perfectly calm way everyone speaks about the next war. It is accepted and taken for granted. All right. Europe has always had wars. But we can keep out of this next one. And the only way to keep out of it is not to go in it; not for any reason. There will be plenty of good reasons. *But we must keep out of it.* If kids want to go to see what war is like, or for the love of

any nation, let them go as individuals. Anyone has a right to go who wants to. But we, as a country, have no business in it and we must keep out.[7]

Later in September, 1935, he devoted a whole letter to a denunciation of war that was subsequently reprinted in the *Reader's Digest*,[8] but his two essential points are made in the passage quoted above.

The first is simply a direct reflection of the isolationist sentiments widespread in the United States in the twenties and thirties. Isolationism took on so many forms and reflected so many motives that it is unsafe to generalize about this movement that culminated in a proposed Constitutional amendment that would have made it impossible for the country to make war, except in the case of invasion, without a national referendum.[9] One of the most literate spokesmen of the movement was Arthur Vandenberg, a newspaperman become Senator from Michigan, the state of which Hemingway often wrote nostalgically in his early stories. Vandenberg probably spoke for all but the lunatic fringe in this country in his analysis of the isolationist (he rejected the term itself) position in *The Trail of a Tradition.*

[Intelligent "Nationalism"] does not require the inculcation of scorns or hatreds or distrusts for other lands and other peoples; it is not a doctrine of external depreciation or destruction. It is a constructive ritual. It seeks maximum friendliness and understanding and self-ordered reciprocal relations with every sector of civilization, no matter what its flag. But it insists that the surrender of American independence is not pre-requisite for those conquests of desirable trans-oceanic amities and of practical international fraternity; nay, more, it insists that the surrender makes the conquest impossible.[10]

Nothing here is out of keeping with the sentiments expressed in Hemingway's *Esquire* pieces; where he parted company with the representative isolationist, however, is apparent in another of Vandenberg's prefatory remarks.

"Nationalism" claims no monopoly of patriotism; but it undertakes to live a patriotism that is effectually faithful. . . . Shall the critical citizen retain unto himself the right to desert his country in the event that her solemn, Constitutional decisions in foreign affairs do not happen to be honored by the validation of his personal, private approval? What essential difference distinguishes him, in such a posture, from the draft-evader who runs away from the colors? As a practical element as discriminated from the individualisms of anarchy—does it not become ultimately necessary for the American's apostrophe to address his country "right or wrong"? Can he retain an option of fidelities? [11]

The politician, covetous of preferment, can have no truck with Hemingway's anarchic concept of "a separate peace," which does demand the exercising of an "option of fidelities," so that the novelist, looking back to Thoreau, perforce marches to "a different drummer" from those who sought to defend the sanctity of national rather than individual policies, even though both agreed to reject "foreign entanglements."

One of the most curious features of Hemingway's viewpoint is discernible in his assertion in the letter from Paris that national isolationism might be coupled with individual interventionism. Hemingway's objection thus is not the pacifist's to violence and war themselves, but to individuals being involved in violence and war without their personal consent. In contradistinction to Vandenberg, Hemingway did indeed feel—as the Existentialists would later—that the individual could be committed only with his "personal, private approval." Hemingway's infatuation with such bloody activities as bullfighting and big game hunting becomes quite understandable when one realizes that he was opposed not to the individual's deliberately flirting with death if he so chose, but to the individual's being manipulated by political forces beyond his personal control.

Hemingway had not come to this philosophy freshly in the thirties; it is dramatized most completely and specifically in the two-part tale, "Big Two-Hearted River," which he assigned the climactic position in his first collection of short stories, significantly titled *In Our Time*. This is also surely the story "about coming back from the war but [with] no mention of the war in it" that, in *A Moveable Feast*, he speaks of completing before starting work on his first novel.[12]

The story begins with Hemingway's familiar *alter ego* Nick returning to a city completely wiped out by a forest fire. Whether one equates this scene of desolation with Western civilization as depicted by T. S. Eliot in *The Waste Land*, or regards it simply as evidence that even spots in America have been blighted by the same ruthless carelessness that has sickened Nick in Europe, the vanished town—upon which the young man turns his back—surely reflects the author's sour view of the urbanized civilization of his time. Nick seeks to escape not only the ruins of the town, but all contacts with human beings. He seeks to reconstruct his own world by observing simple outdoor rituals, because he feels that "he had left everything behind, the need for thinking, the need to write, other needs." [13] Significantly when he reaches the edge of the country that the fire has burned, he strikes off "down the hillside away from the road," ignoring the map and keeping his direction by the sun (as young Ike McCaslin in Faulkner's "The Bear" must divest himself of the accouterments of civilization before he can glimpse the symbol of the unspoiled wilderness). The first section of the story closes with his going to sleep contentedly in the lonely camp that he has made where he wished, as he wished.

The second part of the story is for the most part an almost over-detailed account of an idyllic day's fishing, but the nearly repertorial account is disrupted by two significant evidences that Nick has not left thinking behind after all. The misogynistic attitude that colors the whole work is articulated in the statement, "Nick did not like to fish with other men on the river. Unless they were of your party, they spoiled it." [14] Then the final paragraphs introduce another idea. Coming at last to the place where the river enters a swamp, Nick reflects:

> [He] did not want to go in there now. . . . [I]n the fast deep water, in the half light, the fishing would be tragic. In the swamp fishing was a tragic adventure. Nick did not want it. He did not want to go down the stream any further today.[15]

The very last sentence of the story refers back to this passage: "There were plenty of days coming when he could fish the swamp."

Hemingway's hero manifestly does not intend permanently to eschew "tragic adventure," but he wishes to enter upon it only at the time of his own choosing. It would be difficult to interpret the story, especially in view of Hemingway's penchant for bullfighting and big game hunting, except as the passionate testament of a man who wishes to choose entirely on his own responsibility the moment when, and the conditions under which, he will expose himself to the violence and danger of potentially tragic adventure.

Hemingway's continuing commitment to this egocentric and extraordinarily antisocial philosophy seems to offer the only satisfactory explanation for his enthusiasm over Harry Morgan, the comic-strip hero of *To Have and Have Not* (1935), Hemingway's first novel since *A Farewell to Arms* (1929). For whatever reasons he decided to pad out a story called "One Trip Across" that had appeared in Hearst's *Cosmopolitan* in 1934, the novel may have been intended to show carping critics that Hemingway could write about the depression as well as "the lost generation."

*To Have and Have Not* has never been rapturously

received, although Carlos Baker makes charitable efforts to excuse it on the grounds that Hemingway got caught up in the Spanish War before he could revise it sufficiently. It remains, however, one of the sloppiest novels ever tossed together, one that no author without an established reputation could hope to publish except through a vanity press. Hemingway's sentimental picture of the "have nots," typified by Harry Morgan, a loser with *cojones*, is not, however, as some prissy critics of the thirties tittered, indecent, but simply ludicrous. Critics who find Harry a unique figure simply reveal that they don't follow the exploits of such epic American heroes as Steve Roper. A generally but not completely unsympathetic picture of the debauched "haves" is not integrated into the novel, but simply dumped in occasionally to hold up the narration of the downfall of Morgan. Since this account provides the only thread of interest in the incoherent tale, the author had to take desperate steps to keep what he hoped to offer as a novel from turning back into a short story. Hemingway labors transitional devices in an effort to stress the contrast between "haves" and "have nots," but even assuming that he is making an effort to return to the heavy-handed satire of *The Torrents of Spring*, one can only find the characters stick-figures invented to convey ironic outrage about the injustice of it all.

It still might be difficult to charge the novel with social significance if a repeated circumstance in Harry Morgan's affairs did not dramatize one of the obsessive notions in Hemingway's writings—that of governmental responsibility for the destruction of the modern hero. One may not notice that the first step in Harry's downfall is the result of the American consulate in Havana being closed when Harry needs to take action against a Mr. Johnson who has flown away without paying for the use of Harry's boat, or the loss of valuable fishing gear. The attack on the menace of bureaucracy is unmistakable, however, in the subsequent description of Harry's losing one arm and the boat that he depends upon for his living, as the result of the snooping interference of a personage who describes himself as "one of the three most important men in the United States today" (p. 80).[16] Even though a fishing-boat captain argues that Harry, who is caught dumping bootlegged liquor, has "a family and he's got to eat and feed them," the official makes out an affidavit that leads to Harry's boat being seized and cuts off this independent man's chance to make a living by following his customary trade. Finally when Harry steals his boat back from the Customs service, its hiding place is spotted only because the officious government has begun transporting WPA workers in trucks with unusually high seats.

Hemingway's satire is not all directed, however, at the corrupt capitalistic state, which, besides harassing Harry, underpays Key West's long-suffering native "conches." Harry's death is rather the result of his becoming involved with some starry-eyed radicals who rob a Key West bank in order to finance revolutionary activities in Cuba. Harry Morgan reflects bitterly, after hearing a long spiel by the most amiable looking of the revolutionaries, "To help the working man he robs a bank and kills a fellow works with him and then kills that poor damned Albert that never did any harm. That's a working man he kills. He never thinks of that" (p. 168). And even this young man is obliged to admit the unfortunate effect that the revolutionary effort has had on one of his colleagues, "He is a good revolutionary but a bad man. He kills so much in the time of Machado he gets to like it. He thinks it is funny to kill. He kills in a good cause, of course. The best cause" (p. 158). Surely those who were seeking to overturn decadent democracies could find little encouragement in such writing. Hemingway seems to be justifying anarchic individualism when he puts into the mouth of the rumrunning Harry the words, "I know there ain't no law that you got to go hungry" (p. 96).

Actually the capitalistic system does not fare too badly

in the novel. Although in the twenty-fourth chapter, in which Hemingway surveys the parties aboard the yachts anchored in Key West harbor, he scathingly satirizes heartless speculators and the sycophantish tools of the idle rich that he blasts again in A *Moveable Feast*, he provides a sharply contrasting picture of the happy family of the maker of an overpriced bottled nostrum and of two bleach-headed Esthonians who are sending back to newspapers reports of their intrepid private enterprise in sailing about the world. Although Hemingway may have been satirizing even these self-satisfied folk, he makes their lot appear quite enviable. Despite his attempts to arouse sympathy for the plight of Harry Morgan, the self-made man of the twentieth century, whose last uncomprehended message for the world is "No matter how a man alone ain't got no bloody f——ing chance" (p. 225), Hemingway was never able to put his heart into the effort to castigate those who made their own way by providing the world with pleasant escapes from reality. Whatever he may have intended, the moral of *To Have and Have Not* is best summed up by one of those cynical distortions of traditional wisdom that delighted the jaded 1950's, "Work is the Curse of the Drinking Class."

After this bitter draught, it's small surprise that any writings in which Hemingway espoused a cause like the Spanish Loyalists were received as evidence of a drastic change of heart, so that the nature of Hemingway's partisanship was grossly misconstrued.

As a principal evidence of a change of heart, critics cite *The Spanish Earth*, an artistically masterful propaganda film that Hemingway made in the battle zone in collaboration with the talented Dutch documentary film maker, Joris Ivens. The film itself, however, fails to support the impassioned rhetoric of Jasper Woods in the introduction to the published version of Hemingway's narrative soundtrack.

Until the advent of the invasion of Spain by Franco, Hemingway had never shown any political allegiance, at least not in his writing. But when he saw what was happening to the Spain of many of his short stories and *The Sun Also Rises* and *Death in the Afternoon*, he changed. He expressed his political feelings. He pledged allegiance to the Loyalists, the People's Front, the people who were being invaded and having their lives' work ruined, and those who were not yet old enough to have a life's work having all chances of ever having a life's work destroyed. . . . At first, he faltered in making the final step but when he looked about him and saw most of his friends turning pro-Loyalist and then looked at his beloved Spain and saw its wholesale destruction, he faltered no longer. He took the step full of confidence and devoted his entire self to the salvation of democracy in Spain, his Spain, our Spain, Yes, the people's Spain.[17]

Reading Hemingway's script, one wonders just what picture Woods is talking about. Except for the single opening remark by a peasant, "For fifty years we've wanted to irrigate, but they held us back," [18] and some comments by speakers at a rally to unify the anti-Fascist forces under a single command, there is no debate over the comparative *political* merits of the two sides in the controversy. The point of the picture is rather to protest against the intervention of foreign powers in what the author feels should have remained a civil conflict.

The clearest statement of the writer's viewpoint pays surprising tribute to the men on both sides in the conflict while reflecting, as does another passage about the Italian soldiers at Brihuega, resentment toward those who deny the individual freedom of choice.

Living in the cellars of that ruined building are the enemy. They are Moors and Civil Guards. They are brave troops or they would not have held out after being in a hopeless position. But they are professional soldiers fighting against a people in arms. Trying to impose the will of the military on the will of the people, and the people hate them, for without their tenacity and the constant aid of Italy and Germany, the Spanish revolt would have ended six weeks after it began.[19]

There is no suggestion in the film that other nations should officially intervene on the Loyalist side and convert this provincial struggle into a world conflict. Hemingway hoped rather that the film would inform individual viewers of the true state of things in Spain, so that they would be inspired to offer individual aid, like the members of the International Brigades. Even in this most vigorously propagandistic work, for which he was only partially responsible, Hemingway refused to endorse any cause at the expense of the individual. In some places, like England, however, the author's message was distorted by censors' fearful insistence upon eliminating references to foreign intervention in Spain that gave the picture its only point except as an appalling record of the horrors of warfare.

It is unlikely, too, that the Communist sponsors derived much consolation from Hemingway's appearance before the Second Writers' Congress in New York in 1937. While it is true that Hemingway in his short address to this gathering, which also previewed some footage from *The Spanish Earth*, denounced fascism as the "only one form of government that cannot produce good writers," [20] he again had no positive praise for any system of government. He spoke instead of "friends" who "fight for the freedom of their country against a foreign invasion." [21] The Communists sought to use Hemingway, as they did many writers of the thirties, as a front to advance their own purposes; but Hemingway, far from being duped, appears to have been playing the dangerous game of attempting to use the resources of the Communists to gain support for his personal friends involved in the Spanish conflict. Some of his final remarks to the Writers' Congress appear actually to have been maliciously directed toward quarreling theorists among Leftist intellectuals.

It is very dangerous to write the truth in war and the truth is also very dangerous to come by. I do not know just which American writers have gone out to seek it. . . . Whether the truth is worth some risk to come by, the writers must decide themselves. Certainly it is more comfortable to spend their time disputing learnedly on points of doctrine. And there will always be new schisms and new fallings off and marvelous exotic doctrines and romantic lost leaders, for those who do not want to work at what they profess to believe in, but only to discuss and to maintain positions, skillfully chosen positions with no risk involved in holding them. Positions to be held by the typewriter and consolidated with the fountain pen.[22]

Hemingway's first visit to the Spanish Civil War zone, during which *The Spanish Earth* had been filmed, extended from February to May, 1937. He was back in Spain again between August 14, 1937, and January 28, 1938. During this trip he made his one major effort to treat the Spanish Civil War as a manifestation of class struggle in his only published play, *The Fifth Column*. Even Hemingway's blindest admirers, however, would have difficulty in describing this episodic drama as an "exposé" of the machinations of the "fifth column," the rebel sympathizers within Madrid who collaborated with the four Franco armies pressing on the beleaguered city. In one hysterical conversation, a hotel chambermaid discloses that fifth columnist snipers delight in shooting working people, and a disfigured Communist agent is allowed one speech to explain why the besieged people fight on, "You do it so *every one* will have a good breakfast like that. You do it so *no one* will ever be hungry. You do it so men will not have to fear ill health or old age; so they can live and work in dignity and not as slaves." [23]

The play, however, fails to present any dramatic embodiment of these stirring, often interpolated sentiments; occasionally we see the fleeting figures of fifth columnists, and we hear that vast numbers of them have been rounded up as a result of a cloak-and-dagger raid staged before our eyes, but we are never given any glimpse into the conflicting ideologies of the parties pitted against each other. We are never able to discover why the fifth column exists or how it is able to operate. Despite the misleading title of the work, however, Hemingway cannot be held responsible for the failure of the two sides to confront each other, for he explains in his preface that the play "does not present the nobility and dignity of the cause of the Spanish people," but rather "if it has a moral it is that people who work for certain organizations have very little time for home life." [24]

This uninspiring lesson is presented through the portrayal of the on-again, off-again romance of Philip Rawlings, an American of unspecified background who has become a Red counterespionage agent during a Cuban revolution, and Dorothy Bridges, a Vassar graduate, presumably in Madrid to write Dorothy Thompsonesque articles for Americans seeking enlightenment, but actually engaged principally in smuggling epicurean foods and black-market pesetas. Much of the action churns around their frustrated reflections on what they could be doing if they were not caught up in this messy old war. Since they offer no other clues that they can think, their reflections provide the sole evidence of their basic values; and the spectator can only be appalled by their snobbishness and triviality.

The lovebirds talk mostly about breakfast in bed at luxury resorts like St. Tropez, champagne at twilight in Paris, and cutting people like chic novelist Michael Arlen. One outburst exemplifies their revery.

> Would you like to go to Hungary, too, some fall? You can take an estate there very cheaply and only pay for what you shoot. And on the Danube flats you have great flights of geese. And have you ever been to Lamu where the long white beach is, with the dhows beached on their sides, and the wind in the palms at night? Or what about Malindi where you can surfboard on the beach and the northeast

monsoon cool and fresh, and no pajamas, and sheets at
night. You'd like Malindi.[25]

As one listens to the principal characters in this drama
of a world in flames rattle on like advertisements in
*Holiday*, one cannot resist the suspicion that Hemingway's
real objection to the Spanish Civil War is that it is an
inconvenience to those preoccupied with the pursuit of
novelty. The War had engaged them for a while, as a
fishwives' quarrel might, but it threatens to become a bore.
An author who can present such characters as Philip and
Dorothy, without tongue-in-cheek, and can describe the
latter as an embodiment of "nostalgia," is not really so
much concerned about the plight of the oppressed—in
Hungary, for example—as he is with making the world safe
for the international celebrity set. What actually came out
under fire in Spain is the staggering superficiality of Hemingway's vision of the good life.

The note that links this play to Hemingway's other
works is the sniping throughout at the politician—any
politician. One of the Communist security agents strikes a
chord that resounds throughout Hemingway's work.

> I have seen a politician on the floor in that corner of the
> room unable to stand up when it was time to go out. I have
> seen a politician walk across that floor on his knees and put
> his arms around my legs and kiss my feet. I watched him
> slobber on my boots when all he had to do was such a
> simple thing as die. I have seen many die, and I have never
> seen a politician die well.[26]

Later, the one actual rebel politician that we meet betrays
his own side, although its soldiers prefer to die rather than
betray it. Even the Red Commissar who is so vehement
against other politicians is shown to lie to his own allies,
and to admit complacently that he has mistakenly executed the wrong men.

Hemingway was aware that this portrayal of the unvar-
nished duplicity and blood lust of the Communist agents
would cause his play to be rejected by those fanatical

defenders of the Spanish Republic who could not bear criticism of their side, but he brushed aside such protests with the remark that "fanatics do not make good friends for a cause." [27] He had evidently been annoyed by efforts to make him present the Spanish conflict in strictly black-and-white terms, because he openly discusses, in one of three uncollected stories that he contributed to *Esquire* during the late stages of the Spanish struggle, the matter of what could and should be depicted in tales about the wartime activities of one's own side.

"The Butterfly and the Tank" is set, like the other two stories in this group, in Chicote's once fashionable bar. The story describes the shooting of a poor laboring man for hysterically spraying the waiters with a Flit gun filled with cologne. Those responsible for killing the laborer break out of the restaurant in a phalanx before the police investigation can begin. The narrator then narcissistically gets to the real point of the story, which is to comment upon what a good story he thinks the story that he is telling will make.

> While we were waiting around I told the forceful girl I thought the whole thing was a pretty good story and that I would write it sometime. The way the six had lined up in single file and rushed that door was very impressive. She was shocked and said that I could not write it because it would be prejudicial to the cause of the Spanish Republic. I said that I had been in Spain for a long time and that they used to have a phenomenal number of shootings in the old days around Valencia under the monarchy, and that for hundreds of years before the Republic people had been cutting each other with large knives called Navajas in Andalucia, and that if I saw a comic shooting in Chicote's during the war I could write about it just as though it had been in New York, Chicago, Key West or Marseilles. It did not have anything to do with politics. She said I shouldn't. Probably a lot of other people will say I shouldn't too.[28]

Primarily observer and reporter, Hemingway, in contrast to his critics, was less interested in causes than in drama, more concerned with his own problems as an artist than

with the political expediency of his writings, more interested in the friendship of barflies than recruiting for a
cause. Not even his emotional involvement in the Spanish
Civil War, nor the pressure that friends must have exerted
in an effort to commit him to a more rigidly partisan line,
made a very deep dent in his almost anarchical individualism. He was never really able to conceive of the Spanish
Civil War as a struggle between vast abstract forces; it was
to him that which kept one from enjoying brioches and
jam in St. Tropez; it was the "bad luck" of the hero of
"Old Man at the Bridge." Although this story is Hemingway's shortest evocation of the meaning of the war in
Spain, it is really his most successful, because it conveys
what he found most significant, the frustrating impact of
events upon the isolated individual.

This survey of persistent attitudes underlying Hemingway's writings, both before and during the Spanish War,
points quite directly to the answers to the questions posed
at the beginning of this chapter about *For Whom the Bell
Tolls*, in which the novelist had an opportunity to present
his considered reflections upon the shooting in Spain after
it had stopped.

### iii

The novel depicts in considerable detail the last
seventy-two hours in the life of Robert Jordan, Spanish
teacher at the University of Montana, who has been
touring Spain on a year's leave of absence when the Civil
War breaks out. Jordan has offered his services to the
Loyalists as a dynamiter behind the fascist lines. As the
story opens he has been led by an old Spaniard named
Anselmo to the site of a steel bridge that must be destroyed
to facilitate a Loyalist offensive against Segovia.

To effect the destruction, Jordan joins a group of guerillas, engages in a subtle life-and-death struggle for leadership with the deteriorating head of the band, Pablo ("only
a garbage of what he once was" [p. 284]), and makes love

to Maria, the daughter of a Loyalist mayor, who has been raped and made prisoner after the execution of her parents. Jordan finds the guerillas as suspicious of foreigners as the Extremaduran in "Under the Ridge," and the plans to blow up the bridge are almost frustrated by the opposition of Pablo, who finally throws away the detonators and caps. Jordan himself attempts to call off the explosion and the entire offensive when he discovers that the opposition is aware of the planned attack. Pablo ultimately reconsiders his position and comes back to help carry out the demolition, and Jordan's message arrives too late to halt the offensive. The bridge is destroyed, but Anselmo—Jordan's most valuable helper—is killed by a piece of flying steel. Jordan himself has his leg broken when his horse falls while attempting to cross a road under rebel fire, and he insists that he be left to die while the remnants of the guerilla band escape with Maria.

The novel both opens and closes with pictures of Jordan prone on the pine-needle-covered ground in the most intimate possible association with nature. As the story opens, he has successfully made the trip through the rebel lines and is surveying the opposition that he must overcome to destroy the bridge; as the story closes, he is sinking into unconsciousness, but hopes, with the machine gun that he has poised, to carry to death with him the first rebel horseman to appear. He is in the same physical position at other times in the story, particularly on two significant occasions late in the narrative: first when Maria, as a result of their sexual relationship, is transported into *la gloria*, and again as he waits for the first signs of daylight to launch the attack on those defending the bridge.

The insistent emphasis at key points in the novel upon this virtual integration of man into nature, suggests that Hemingway may have been writing a kind of primitivistic idyll in which an equation is made between the loyalist camp and the pine-needled goodness of Nature, on the one hand, and the rebel-held bridge and the mechanical evils of civilization on the other. The destruction of the bridge would thus not be simply one necessary part of a Loyalist offensive, but a symbolic step toward the restoration of a natural order. Allen Guttmann has on several occasions shown in great detail the way in which "for Hemingway, the Spanish Civil War, was, among other things, a struggle waged by men close to the earth and to the values of a primitive society against men who had turned away from the earth, men who had turned to the machine and to the antithetical values of an aggressive and destructive mechanical order." [29] Guttmann argues that the book is in "the very *American*" tradition of Cooper's Natty Bumppo and Huck Finn.

*For Whom the Bell Tolls* is not, however, a simple back-to-nature tale. For Hemingway, as for Steinbeck, machinery is not so much evil in itself as it is in the hands of evil men. Despite his affection for the backwoods, Hemingway is not a Luddite. As Robert Jordan waits for the dawn of what will be his last day, he reflects, "If the French help at all, if only they leave the frontier open and if we get planes from America they can never finish with us. Never, if we get anything at all. These people will fight forever if they're well armed" (p. 432). He has no illusions about the hill folk wiping out the fascists with their bare hands.

Hemingway, furthermore, never expresses a faith in a beneficent nature. Capricious and undependable, nature often sets man's best laid plans at naught. In *A Farewell to Arms*, Frederic Henry, after he makes his separate peace and manages to escape his human foes at the bridge where he is threatened by a kangaroo court and at the Swiss border, is ultimately defeated by the uncontrollable forces of nature. His child is strangled by its umbilical cord, and Catherine dies of hemorrhages. Henry walks off alone into the pervasive rain, cut off from both the world of society that he has rejected and the private world that he and Catherine have constructed to take its place. The same nature that provided him with the floating log that made possible his escape from the carbinieri and that provides the guerilla band in *For Whom the Bell Tolls* with the overhanging ledge that protects it from air surveillance, is capable of freakish behavior that brings down the refuges that men seeking autonomy create for themselves.

The climactic vagary of nature in *For Whom the Bell Tolls* is the May snowstorm, which Hemingway specifically describes as a "freak." When this storm discloses the hiding place of El Sordo and his guerillas, the entire band that Jordan counted on for reinforcements is destroyed. Throughout the later pages of the story, Jordan and the other characters dilate at length upon what Pilar calls the beautiful but rotten snow that has given events a tragic turn (p. 154). The success of the attack on the bridge is endangered not only by jealousy and inefficiency within the military command, but by the unpredictability of nature. In *For Whom the Bell Tolls*, as in *A Farewell to Arms*, the individual man cannot turn to either society or nature with any expectation of dependable assistance. Certainly the Spanish War did not cause Hemingway to abandon the concept of the utter isolation of the individual that had run through his earlier writings.

Actually *For Whom the Bell Tolls* is structurally a curious variation on the pattern of *A Farewell to Arms*. Alvah Bessie, veteran of the International Brigades, in one of the angriest reviews of the novel argues that Hemingway treats the Spanish War in it "exactly as he treated the first world war in *A Farewell to Arms*" because of "its destruction of everything all decent human beings value." [30] In his wrath, however, Bessie failed to notice that although in both novels Hemingway does indeed express the same view toward war as a social or political instrument, he switches the self-asserted relationship of the protagonist to the conflict. Whereas the disillusioned Frederic Henry at last declares "a separate peace," the more sophisticated Robert Jordan attempts to carry on "a separate war." He attempts to fight alongside the Loyalists without becoming more than technically associated with them.

Although in his conversations with the Spaniards, Jordan talks about fighting for the "cause," he makes clear in an early conversation with Maria that he is not a Communist, but an "anti-fascist" (p. 66). Even earlier, in a passage reminiscent of Marlow in Joseph Conrad's *Heart of Darkness*, Jordan has told Pilar, the guerilla leader's mate, that he believes in his "work" as a dynamiter, not his efforts for some abstract cause (p. 33). He is willing to act under the direction of the Communists, for he feels that in Spain they "offered the best discipline and the soundest and sanest for the prosecution of the war" (p. 163), and discipline is needed to win the war. He refuses, however, to align himself ideologically with the Communists, choosing rather to suspend his judgment.

> who censored his thinking? Nobody but himself. He would not think himself into any defeatism. The first thing was to win the war. If we did not win the war everything was lost. But he noticed, and listened to, and remembered everything. He was serving in a war and he gave absolute loyalty and as complete performance as he could give while he was serving. But nobody owned his mind, nor his faculties for seeing and hearing, and if he were going to form judgments he would form them afterwards. (pp. 135–36)

Later he reflects that, though he would not tell anyone else, he, like old Anselmo, has "no politics." He is willing to accept the Communist discipline, which he respects, for the duration of the war because he has no positive program for after the victory. He only feels that "If the Republic lost it would be impossible for those who believed in it to live in Spain" (p. 163).

When importuned, however, to identify himself more firmly with the Communist cause, he replies, "My mind is in suspension until we win the war" (p. 245). The concept of a "separate war" rather than a "separate peace" makes it possible for Hemingway to turn his novel into an attack

upon those who refuse to help idealistic youth win the
battles it believes in, rather than upon those like the
sloganeers in A Farewell to Arms that have led youth into
a war that it does not understand. Actually Hemingway's
concept is only an individualized version of what James P.
Warburg calls "the isolationist illusion"—that a country
can "if it chooses, dissociate itself from the affairs of the
world." [31] Such an illusion can be maintained, however, in
its pristine purity, only in very special circumstances—only
as long as two oceans effectively isolated the United States
from the rest of the world or as long as Robert Jordan
could be away from the main body of troops, the constant
supervision of military superiors, and the constant propaganda bombardment from "information" officers. It is not
surprising that when talking with Pilar and El Sordo about
what to do after the destruction of the bridge necessitates
the movement of the guerilla band, Jordan argues that
they should go to another place behind the lines, although
Pilar wishes to cross the lines and rejoin the main body of
the Republican forces.

Jordan wishes to keep his war physically as well as
ideologically "separate," because he realizes that when he is
in Madrid, enjoying the comparative comforts of hotels
and restaurants even in a besieged city, he is tempted to
succumb to the blandishments of the Communists who
would like to command not just his services but also his
soul. Back where the leaders gather, he reflects:

> You felt, in spite of all bureaucracy and inefficiency and
> party strife something that was like the feeling you expected
> to have and did not have when you made your first com-
> munion. It was a feeling of consecration to a duty toward all
> of the oppressed of the world which would be as difficult
> and embarrassing to speak about as religious experience.
> . . . It gave you a part in something that you could be-
> lieve in wholly and completely and in which you felt an
> absolute brotherhood with the others who were engaged
> in it. (p. 235)

Reflecting on the way a clever Russian journalist has led him to accept Communist rationalizations of expediencies, Jordan thinks wryly to himself, "You corrupt very easily," but then he wonders, "But was it corruption or was it merely that you lost the naïveté that you started with. Would it not be the same in anything? Who else kept that first chastity of mind about their work that young doctors, young priests, and young soldiers usually started with?" (p. 239).

He is never able to answer this question or to decide whether he really prizes such chastity; but, although he advises the rebels to continue to operate behind the lines almost to the very end of the story, he himself dreams of returning to Madrid with Maria in order to hobnob with the bigwigs and to take part in lofty discussions again. Although Hemingway might have been reluctant to admit it, Jordan's naïveté lies really in his illusion that one can, like a mechanized "Lone Ranger," fight a "separate war" that demands involvement, at least, with the enemy forces even by taking the infinite pains necessary to maintain a "separate peace." Jordan embodies the schizophrenic feelings of a man like Hemingway who distrusted organized society and hated being involved in a war without his personal consent, while at the same time loving some particular place like Spain—that involved him emotionally in a particular war—and being attracted to the "controlled violence" of bullfighting or big game hunting. A letter that Hemingway wrote Carlos Baker in 1951 about his affection for Spain and his lack of politics, confirms the suspicion that the novelist became caught up in the drift of world affairs only because the battleground for the major rehearsal turned out to be his beloved Spain.[32]

Alvah Bessie objects in his review of *For Whom the Bell Tolls* that the novel is not about Spain, but he is wrong. The Spanish people, the Spanish countryside pervade every page of the book. Bessie would be correct, however, if he said what he probably really meant, that the novel is not about the Spanish Civil War as an ideological conflict. It is the report by a man who loves Spain of something terrible that has happened there. But anyone who turns to Hemingway's novel for any clear account of the situation that resulted in the outbreak of the war, of the motivations of the two sides in the conflict, or of the ideological positions the contenders symbolized is going to be disappointed and quite possibly confused.

I certainly do not mean to imply that Hemingway should have turned his novel into some kind of introduction to the causes of the war—a novel is not a textbook. Some critics have, however, continually treated the novel as though it did tell us something about the War and the issues it involved rather than about Hemingway's highly individualistic enthusiasms and philosophy; and Hemingway himself has compounded the confusion by taking us occasionally, during the course of the novel, out of Robert Jordan's mind and offering us, particularly during the account of the guerilla Andrés's trip to General Golz's headquarters, a highly colored view of particular individuals influential in the conduct of the war. The objection to the inclusion of material like the devastating attacks upon the paranoid French Communist leader Marty is not that there may be no basis for them, but that they belong in a letter to *Esquire* rather than in *For Whom the Bell Tolls* because they tend to convert the moving account of Robert Jordan's struggles with the world and himself into name-calling journalism.

Once the wealth of detail has been cut away from the skeleton of its structure, *For Whom the Bell Tolls* can be seen like *Pilgrim's Progress* as another tale of "one man's journey" through a sorry world, and this journey ends as all such journeys had ended in Hemingway's earlier novels with the hero either dead or utterly disillusioned while the wicked flourished (Hemingway casts even himself in this role of victim in his account in A *Moveable Feast* of his seduction by the rich). Hemingway's viewpoint is summed up in the cheerless words of T. S. Eliot's Gerontion, "what is kept must be adulterated."

We can answer now, I think, the three questions with which I launched this discussion. Hemingway does undeniably emphasize the brutality of the Loyalist forces in the novel. One of the things that principally outraged pro-Loyalists like Alvah Bessie was the amount of space the novelist devoted, for example, to Pilar's gruesomely graphic account of Pablo's destruction of the Fascists in his native village (pp. 103–26). Similar behavior on the part of the Rebels is indicated, of course, in the description of their treatment of the Republicans in Maria's village (pp. 165, 350–53) and even in Pilar's remark that the slaughter of the Fascists was "the worst days of my life until one other" that came "three days later when the Fascists took the town" (p. 129). But these horrors are not described in as great detail, so that the reader is left with the sharpest impression of the barbarity of the Loyalists.

Nor are they accused only of brutality. The corruption of their leaders is exposed (pp. 229–30), suppression of evidence of Russian intervention is mentioned (p. 237), their manufacturing of "peasant leaders" because a real one "might have too many peasant characteristics" is pointed out (p. 229), their stupidity is stressed in the misinterpretation of the firing that destroys El Sordo's camp, as dissension among the rebels (p. 357), and Pablo is finally exposed as a murderer who destroys the men on his own side whom he recruits to help him (p. 455). Robert Jordan is even obliged sadly to recognize, "You were fighting against exactly what you were doing and being forced into doing to have any chance of winning" (p. 162). Because we see far more of the Loyalists, they look even worse than the Fascists; and indeed one of the few relatively decent characters in the book is the rebel

Lieutenant Paco Berrendo, at whom Jordan is leveling his gun as the novel ends.

Thus a black picture is painted of the Loyalists, but since the War was over nothing could be accomplished by falsely glamorizing them except to lay the groundwork for a sentimental myth. Hemingway's point is his old one that all warfare is vicious and dehumanizing; it brings out the worst in one's own side as well as the other side. The danger, Robert Jordan feels, is that when one begins killing, he may—like the revolutionary in *To Have and Have Not*—come to believe in it and then "the whole thing is wrong" (p. 304). Probably, however, Hemingway overcolored his story because he had his eye on his immediate audience.

So much had already been heard in the United States about the atrocities committed by Franco's forces and so firmly had Hemingway been identified with the Loyalists, that he probably felt it necessary to redress the balance if the novel were to make his point about the superiority of the individual to the cause. He could assume in 1940 that most of his readers would be familiar, for example, with the internationally denounced rebel raid on the Basque city of Guernica. Impressed by the power of Pilar's story-telling, Robert Jordan even reflects, "What we did. Not what the others did to us. He knew enough about that" (pp. 134–35). In his elegy for fallen Spain, Hemingway wished, not to aggravate the division that had prostrated the country, but to emphasize the degrading effects of war on both sides. Thus his book stands in this regard as in others as a poignant piece of antiwar propaganda, and yet an especially curiously one-sided account of the war to those who had not lived through the years of the struggle themselves, but who had heard of the author's Loyalist sympathies.

The probable reasons for placing the action behind the lines in the camp of an isolated guerilla band have already been suggested. Only in such a location could a man be able at all to maintain the illusion of carrying on a kind of "separate war"; as part of the main body of the Loyalist army Robert Jordan would inevitably either have become the tool that he made of others or else he would have dissipated his energies in fruitless controversies that would have very likely led to his early execution. War is, furthermore, a simpler thing in the simple setting of a guerilla camp than it can be in a complex military or civilian society. Jordan himself learns something of the complexity of the situation in Madrid. It is not possible to make clearcut, absolute judgments of people and their motives in a crowded, beleaguered city full of agents and counteragents; but behind the lines, Hemingway points out early in the novel, "You had to trust the people you worked with completely or not at all" (p. 4). By choosing the setting that he did, Hemingway relieved himself of the problem of coping with the complexities of fixing responsibility in a military hierarchy that has caused even such effective works as Norman Mailer's *The Naked and the Dead* and Joseph Heller's *Catch-22* to become collections of brilliant fragments rather than well unified presentations of a consistent theme.[33]

Behind the lines, working with a small group, one can also learn to know and to handle each member of the group as an individual, and it is individuals rather than anonymous masses that interested Hemingway. Considering the way the author depicts the discipline at the Loyalist front, both the gypsy who abandons his post to hunt rabbits and Pablo, after he throws away the detonators, would have been summarily executed. But in a small band, men are too scarce and valuable to be shot without a consideration of individual motivations that may lead one to forgive or at least to tolerate. Significantly, when Jordan does get away from the guerillas, he seeks to pal around with the high brass in Madrid, to move in circles where he can also recognize and learn to understand each man as an individual. As critics have often observed, Hemingway is an artist of the personal, and he could treat of individual personalities in a war novel only by confining his action to some kind of extremely small or isolated group.

There is finally the problem of the suspiciously contrived death of the American dynamiter. Artistically, of course, the accident that breaks Robert Jordan's leg makes it possible for Hemingway to present a heart-rending final irony in which two of the finest representatives of the opposing forces, Jordan and Lieutenant Berrendo, destroy each other, while the rascally Pablo sneaks away. Such an ending would be suitable for a short story denouncing war, but hardly adequate for a novel of the length and complexity of *For Whom the Bell Tolls*. Hemingway had more compelling reasons for needing to get Robert Jordan out of the way.

First, as I have already suggested, Hemingway was not prepared to let Jordan discover the whole answer to his question about his own chastity and corruption. Since Hemingway was writing the novel after the conclusion of the conflict, Jordan's survival would have implied his ultimate compromise with corruption. The only way in which Hemingway could keep his hero untarnished was to have him go down with the side whose survival he had equated with the survival of decency in Spain. Yet Hemingway could not have his hero kill himself to preserve his scruples, as J. D. Salinger, for example, could later have his Seymour Glass do, because Hemingway endowed Jordan, whose father had—like Hemingway's—committed suicide, with an obsessive horror of self-destruction as cowardly.

Yet although Jordan has a horror of suicide, he is motivated by a death-wish. Although he is inhibited from hoping for his own destruction, he does openly express his unwillingness to perpetuate the race when he tells Maria, "I would not wish to bring either a son or a daughter into this world as this world is" (p. 354). Hemingway makes it clear that the future cannot lie in the hands of this scholarly observer who has chosen to fight for a foreign people. Jordan's unwillingness to father children is a corollary to the lack of commitment that distinguishes him throughout the novel; he is willing to work for those that he loves who have had the misfortune to be born, but he is unwilling to take any responsibility for shaping the future. In a sense, except as a technician, he is dead long before his physical death.

But why does Hemingway choose to employ as his principal figure this character whose defeat has been inevitable from the beginning—just as the defeat of the Republic was already a reality when the novel was written? He is all the things which Hemingway believes that the world should value. He is sensitive to other people; he is a keen and sympathetic observer; he appreciates the good things in life, which in this novel are described as being considerably less shoddy than in *The Fifth Column* (Robert Jordan reflects that one small cup of absinthe takes the place "of the evening papers, of all the old evenings in cafés, of all chestnut trees that would be in bloom now in this month, of the great slow horses of the outer boulevards, of book shops, of kiosques, and of galleries." [p. 51]).

Such a person, Hemingway feels, is doomed by a society that has been corrupted beyond hope of recovery by stultifying abstractions. Actually the whole course of the novel and its hero's life are foreshadowed in one of old Anselmo's first speeches: "This is the easy country of the pass where the stream flows gently. Below, where the road turns out of sight in the trees, it drops suddenly and there is a steep gorge———" (p. 1). Jordan, who longs for the pleasant life in the easy country, has been plunged into the last and steepest gorge of his short life.

Thus the bell tolls for Robert Jordan and the Spanish Republic. Alvah Bessie and other critics have generally assumed that the Donne quotation which Hemingway borrowed refers to some kind of "universal brotherhood of man," with *brotherhood* meaning a formal association of some kind. Donne's use of the phrase "no man is an *Iland*" justifies this fraternalistic interpretation, but Hemingway's novel made critics feel—I think correctly—that the novelist was not thinking of individual man merging his identity into some kind of order or cause.

One can have a feeling of brotherhood without the encumbrance of creeds and party lines, without the surrender of the control of one's thinking. The clearest notion of Hemingway's concept of the "brotherhood of man" occurs not in any of those passages in which Robert Jordan recalls the Communists' rationalizations of their behavior in "destroying" obstructionists, but in the rascally Pablo's speech when, after throwing away the dynamite detonators, he returns to the band, "after I had thrown away thy material I found myself too lonely." He goes on to explain to Pilar, "I do not like to be alone. *Sabes?* Yesterday all day alone working for the good of all I was not lonely. But last night. *Hombre! Qué mal lo páse!*" (pp. 390–91).[34] The man who cuts himself off from the group suffers the horrors of loneliness.

This is the message that Hemingway had for his American readers. He was not writing a book like Sinclair Lewis' *It Can't Happen Here*, warning that fascism could overtake America, even though he observed that there were fascistic tendencies in this country. Nor did he argue that the United States government should have intervened in the Spanish War. He believed that it should simply have permitted help to reach the Loyalists. His attack was directed especially at those like the two brothers in the guerilla camp who feel no commitment to the group and would just as soon have been Fascists if their father had been, because "it was easier to live under a regime than to fight it" (p. 367). His belief was that those who wished to make a choice should have the right to make it ("I believe in the people and their right to govern themselves as they wish," Robert Jordan reflects [p. 304]), and his point was that with the death of Republican Spain the men of conscience in the United States had sacrificed others who might have worked with them for the good of all.

We can see another reason now for Hemingway's concentrating on the excesses of the Loyalist forces. He was making precisely the same point that Steinbeck stresses in *The Grapes of Wrath*—one should assist people not because they are virtuous, but simply because they aspire to human dignity. The Spanish Loyalists have serious, even grave defects; they may offend fastidious tastes and appear to live like beasts; but a United States that tolerates the kind of lynching which Jordan saw in his childhood (p. 116) has no occasion to patronize others who surrender under pressure to bestial passions. If, furthermore, these people are to be sacrificed because they have small imperfections, those who have refused to succor them are going to be awfully lonely. We cannot expect those who appeal to us in dire emergencies to cool their heels until we examine their references.

Yet despite his feeling that men of good will must assist each other, Hemingway had by no means overcome his profound suspicions of any governmental hierarchy. He still felt that, although one might have to commit one's self temporarily to the lesser of two evil governments to achieve some specific goal, all politics corrupt and ultimately destroy the individual.

He had not in the final analysis lost any of the suspicions of high-sounding abstractions that Frederic Henry expresses in *A Farewell to Arms*. He did not insist that the Spanish Republic should have been helped in the sacred name of liberty or justice; he resorted rather to the individual's primitive fear of being left all alone and he extolled through his portrait of Robert Jordan, the individual who was willing to sacrifice himself rather than permit others to suffer the fate of the abandoned.

*For Whom the Bell Tolls* is thus truly the work of an author, like its principal character, "without politics."

Hemingway gained his reputation as a visceral writer, one whose sensory reporting appeals directly to the reader's feelings. Indeed he himself explained in his address to the Second Writers' Congress that he thought it was the writer's problem to project the truth "in such a way that it becomes a part of the experience of the person who reads it." [35] In A *Moveable Feast*, he describes something of the way in which he wrote.

> When I stopped writing I did not want to leave the river where I could see the trout in the pool, its surface pushing and swelling smooth against the resistance of the log-driven piles of the bridge. . . . But in the morning the river would be there and I must make it and the country and all that would happen.[36]

Throughout his career Hemingway remained the kind of extraordinarily successful reporter who was able to "make things happen"—to re-create the very feeling of an experience in the responsive reader.[37] Unfortunately, in choosing for his two novels of the thirties titles suggestive of intellectual positions of the time, he left the impression that he had arrived at some kind of explicable philosophical basis for taking sides in some of the era's most pressing controversies. *For Whom the Bell Tolls*, although set against a background of one of the most convulsive struggles between freedom and tyranny in the thirties, is scarcely a social novel at all in the restricted definition that I am employing in this study, because it sheds little light on the motivations behind the particular political events it concerns. Rather it repeats simply the ancient human truth that man hates to be alone. Yet paradoxically the novel continues to be regarded as one of the principal efforts in American fiction to shed light on a particular sequence of events, while Faulkner's *The Hamlet*, which sheds so much light on particular events, continues to be regarded principally as an epic embodiment of ancient human truths.

# 5 SALVATION SQUADS: COMMISSAR AND CROSS

DALTON TRUMBO'S NAME has twice figured prominently in the news since the apparent close of his career as a novelist. He was first unwillingly shoved into prominence in 1947 as one of the most vocal of the "Hollywood Ten," who ultimately served jail sentences because of their unwillingness to testify about their Communist affiliations to the House of Representatives Committee on Un-American Activities.

Under the chairmanship of New Jersey representative J. Parnell Thomas, who went to jail himself for payroll padding at about the same time as some of the unfriendly moviemakers, the Committee decided to investigate Communist infiltration of the influential film industry. A subcommittee headed by Thomas himself arrived in Hollywood on May 9, 1947, to conduct preliminary hearings. Trumbo's name came up on the first day when Mrs. Leila Rogers testified that he had tried to insert into the picture *Tender Comrade*, a Communistic sentiment that her daughter Ginger refused to utter.[1] When the full committee hearings began back in Washington in October, Trumbo's name was again one of the first mentioned, this time by producer Sam Wood, President of the Motion Picture Alliance for the Preservation of American Ideals.[2]

Trumbo was called before the Committee on October 29. When he refused to answer any questions about

Communist ties and tried to read a statement into the record denouncing the investigation, he was cited for contempt of Congress. On December 3, a week after top film executives reluctantly decided to suspend those who refused to testify before the committee, Trumbo was fired by Metro-Goldwyn-Mayer; on December 12, following the investigation by a District of Columbia grand jury, he was taken into custody, and in May, 1948, he was convicted, fined, and sentenced to a year in prison, although as the result of a series of appeals finally reaching the United States Supreme Court, he did not begin to serve the sentence until July, 1950.

Although after the group's imprisonment director Edmund Dmytryk confessed his Communist affiliations, denounced the party, and returned to work, Trumbo remained silent. Following his release from prison, he seemed simply to disappear from the scene, banished from his profession.

Before the fifties ended, however, Trumbo made news once more. When the Academy Awards for 1956 were passed out, the one for an original screenplay went to a Robert Rich, who failed to appear to claim it. Later in 1957, Trumbo announced during an interview over a Los Angeles television station that he had been working for several years under pseudonyms, bootlegging scripts to Hollywood studios, and that he had even been nominated several times for Academy Awards. He refused, however, to identify himself as Rich. Although a number of claimants for the award did come forward, their claims were disallowed and the matter was largely forgotten until 1960 when the problem of what to do about those who had refused to testify about Communist affiliations again arose in connection with the Academy's proceedings. After it was disclosed that one of the nominees for scriptwriting would be ineligible under the rule denying awards to those who had declined to testify, the Academy of Motion

Picture Arts and Sciences decided in January, 1960, to abandon the rule as unworkable.

After this decision, Trumbo at last identified himself as Rich. Later the same month, producer Otto Preminger publicly announced that he had hired Trumbo as Trumbo to write the script for the superspectacle to be based on Leon Uris's best-selling novel *Exodus*, and Universal-International studios was reportedly mulling over whether or not to give Trumbo screen credit for collaborating on the script for the equally spectacular *Spartacus*, based on a Howard Fast novel. After much hesitation, the studio awarded the credit. Except for some picketing by the American Legion at the premier of *Exodus*, the producers suffered none of the dreaded repercussions that they had feared they might for embracing an alleged subversive, and Trumbo has since remained out of the news and in Hollywood making money.

During the controversy over his political activities, participants generally overlooked the fact that he at one time had pretensions as an artist; so greatly have the activities that made Trumbo notorious overshadowed his earlier work that there does not appear previously to have been any assessment of the purely literary merits of the four novels that he published between 1935 and 1941. Conceivably they have been neglected because of a lack of permanent merit; but Trumbo should not be ignored in any consideration of the social novel at the end of the thirties. He dealt more vehemently than most writers with some of the most aggravating social situations of these years, and his later celebrity adds special interest to his work as evidence of the thinking of the discontented.

Possibly the rancor that characterizes Trumbo's fiction is at least partly attributable to his difficulties in getting a start. Born in Montrose, Colorado, in 1905, he worked for years at such menial jobs as bread-wrapping before he cracked the commercial writers' market in his late twenties. He was thirty before his first fiction was published; his earlier articles had dealt critically with the subject that always most preoccupied him, Hollywood, whose "tragedy," he maintained, "lies in the fact that its masters were as ignorant of the fundamental causes of their success as its enemies." [3]

His first novel, *Eclipse*, was published by an obscure London firm in 1935 and never appears to have been reprinted anywhere. Although it fails to develop any consistent theme, this little-known book shows that Trumbo knew the techniques of his craft far better than most first novelists. It is of interest, too, for its foreshadowing of ideas and situations that reappear in his work.

*Eclipse* tells the story of the effects of the advent of the depression on John Abbott, whose vision, energy, and money have been largely responsible for the growth of Shale City, Colorado, a thriving town situated much like Grand Junction where Trumbo grew up. The story begins when Abbott is sixty and at the peak of both his affluence and influence as town patron.

When the depression strikes, however, Abbott learns how short men's memories are. He is personally blamed, when his ventures falter, for all the evils that have befallen this town that over-extended itself, and he is snubbed and reviled by the very people who previously courted his favor. His long cultivated reputation has indeed been eclipsed, and the moral of the novel is that men are ingrates. This point is made in a conversation in the antepenultimate chapter between Abbott, who dazed by his fall from fortune has been wandering down by the river's side, and a hardy old woman who dwells there; she advises Abbott to quit banking. He asks her what he might do then.

> "Oh," her voice was vague, "don't make a hell of a lot of difference. A body don't need much. Just a few things."
> "What are they?"
> "Well, you got to have a shack, and something to fill your

belly, and somebody to go to bed with now and then. That's about all."

He nodded, "Nothing else?"

"Well, some folks want more. Now take you. You did. You wanted banks and such-like. I just wanted a shack and some grub and my old man. You had what you wanted, but you ain't got it now. But me—I ain't never lost mine. Nobody else wanted to git it off'n me." [4]

If the book concluded with this conversation, it would be a fairly straightforward primitivist comment on the vanity of human wishes; but it is not clear whether Abbott's subsequent return to town to burn down his department store, while moaning his dead mistress's name, represents an effort at purgation or a dying effort to make an impression on the community.

*Eclipse*'s lack of dramatic consistency results, however, from Trumbo's succumbing even this early in his career to the temptation that would reduce his novels to tracts—the interpolation into the narrative of long, violent harangues by mysterious cynics. These are delivered in *Eclipse* by Hermann Vogel, a refugee of unfathomed background from Imperial Austria-Hungary, who is the local history teacher and "beyond all doubt" the town's cleverest man. This exotic bird appears on only three occasions to lecture Abbott for several pages: first, on the town's ex-Loyalty Leaguers some day turning on Abbott, although they then fawn on him; later, on a man's need for a sexual outlet, and finally, on the need for more prolific childbearing to increase the nation's consumer power. Unless Vogel, who is never treated satirically, is Trumbo's spokesman, it is hard to guess what he is doing in the book, because he is never involved in the action. His speeches seem grafted onto the story, because the ideas in them are not—like those in the interchapters in *The Grapes of Wrath*—dramatized in the main plot. Even when the town finally turns on Abbott, it is not for the reasons Vogel foreshadowed, although it is significant that Trumbo's own subsequent difficulties arose from his nonconformist attitudes.

One of Vogel's tirades is also especially significant in view of the author's later work and activities. In a sarcastic outline of the United States' participation in the first World War, Vogel foreshadows the virulent pacifism of *Johnny Got His Gun* and *The Remarkable Andrew:* "Well America got into it, too. . . . Oh God, what fun! May no one ever forget how we elected Wilson because he kept us out of war. May they never forget, and may the dead forgive them." In the same speech Trumbo suggests that his surly attitude before the Congressional investigating committee had deep roots, when he has Vogel rail that the Loyalty League represented "the power of snoopery, persecution, investigation," which "no one dared oppose . . . because no one dared risk the charge of treason." [5]

Although Vogel's speeches all leave the implication that Abbott, who like Faulkner's Flem Snopes is sterile, is a victim of a vicious society, Trumbo also writes that Abbott's wife is "the one person in Shale City who knew that her husband's public spirit grew from the poverty of his own soul." [6] This suggests that Abbott's tragedy is the fault of his own vaulting ambition, so that it is not clear why society should finally have treated him differently from what it did. *Eclipse* is an angry book, but Trumbo seems not to know really why he is angry. Society becomes a convenient scapegoat for the author's inability to be tough enough with the characters that he has created.

This inability is even more marked in Trumbo's second novel, an attempted satire on bureaucracy; but before looking at *Washington Jitters* (1936), we need to be aware of some other developments in Trumbo's fast-breaking career. In the same year that *Eclipse* appeared, Trumbo finally cracked the slick fiction market by placing two short stories in the *Saturday Evening Post* [7] that show the writer's ability to create the same kind of slangy dialogue, raffish characters, and ironic surprise endings that had made Damon Runyon famous. Both stories show, like a chapter in *Eclipse* that deals with converting a reluctant prostitute into a housemaid for the town's Carrie Nation, that Trumbo had a talent for creating fast-moving, compli-cated, but essentially trivial tales—a gift that would serve him well in writing for the motion pictures.

When he attempted, however, to expand one of these tales into a novel, the strain on the fragile material became too great. *Washington Jitters* is simply a collection of the tired anti-New Deal clichés that circulated during the thirties, about the officiousness and bumbling inefficiency of bureaucracy and the menace of scheming newspaper columnists. Like many ephemeral works of that spite filled period, the novel draws much of its humor from catty portraits of thinly disguished luminaries, like this one suggested by Upton Sinclair, who was then pushing his E.P.I.C. plan to end poverty in California.

> The lean, nervous, white-haired radical who had spent his most productive years valorously squabbling with the beef, oil, and money trusts darted forward, pecked at Henry's hand, and just as suddenly let it drop as if it might be a trifle filthy. He retired to his original position a little apart from the others, where he remained, his face twitching into swift little smiles as the conversation veered and turned.[8]

The novel tells the not particularly original story of the rise of a little man to political eminence through a misun-derstanding. He falls into the hands of a group of schem-ing demagogues who plan to nominate him as a third-party candidate for President. Henry perceives, however, that they intend to exploit him for their own purposes; and in a scene that provides release for every adolescent's fantasy of reviling his oppressors, this particular worm turns.

> "You all think that I'm a fool. I've suspected it for a long time, and after this meeting I know it. You've taken me for a fool, and I've got a surprise for you. Know what it

is? . . . I'm *not* a fool! I see what you're planning to do with me, and I'm not going to stand for it. You're a bunch of fakers. I don't need you. I never did need you. I was making a decent living before I met any of you, and I'll be making a decent living long after I've forgotten you." [9]

But the novel does not end on this high note. As in Trumbo's other fiction, the virtuous hero is ultimately crushed by the irresistible forces of a vicious system. At the end of the book, as Henry sails off to Europe as an administration hireling, he says tragically, "I'm not a signpainter any more. I'm not even a man. I'm nothing but a politician . . . ." [10]

The novel is not tragic, however, because Trumbo never convinces the reader that Henry—like John Abbott in *Eclipse*—is anything more than an opportunist with no basically higher ideals than his exploiters. Trumbo simply expects us to believe in his little man because he is a little man. Trumbo's tragedy, therefore, is simply a sentimental effusion over mediocrity finding its own level, and his comedy degenerates into a vicious *roman à clef* aimed spitefully at transient celebrities. Even the few reviewers of the period who noticed *Washington Jitters* dismissed it casually as light fiction, and even the sponsorship of the influential Theatre Guild failed to keep a play version alive longer than three weeks on Broadway.

Despite his unimpressive showing in traditional media, Trumbo was beginning to win recognition as a screenwriter. The same year of 1935 that saw the publication of his first novel and short stories found him at last breaking into the hard-to-enter but well-paid ranks of screenwriters. He signaled his success with a special boldface announcement in the *Film Daily Year Book* that he had worked on scripts for *Young Nowheres*, *Gild-Edged Blonde*, and *Road Gang*. The first two of these ventures apparently never reached the screen, but in 1936 *Road Gang's* credits flashed Trumbo's name on theater screens throughout the country. That year he also collaborated with Tom Reed on the script for *Love Begins at Twenty* and sold the original story for *Tugboat Princess*. In 1937 he worked at Columbia Studios with Liam O'Flaherty and Jerome Chodorov on the most ambitious production with which he had so far been connected, *Devil's Playground*, a tale about Navy deep-sea divers, starring several fading screen luminaries: Chester Morris, Dolores Del Rio, and Richard Dix. The next year he began an association with RKO Studios that was to last during the five years that he attracted most attention as a writer.

The thirties were the heyday of the "B" picture, a trivial, inexpensive entertainment, ground out in quantity to provide fillers for double-feature programs, or theaters presenting stage shows. During the period that Trumbo worked at RKO, Anne Shirley was the local "B" queen, and for her he wrote such scripts as *Sorority House* and *Career*. One of the "B" pictures, made in collaboration with director Garson Kanin, then new to the screen, proved a surprising critical success. This picture, *A Man to Remember*, afforded Trumbo at last the opportunity to reach a wider and more impressionable audience with the same kind of story that he had told in *Eclipse* of a community's failure to appreciate the efforts of a leading citizen, this time a doctor, who had devoted his life to the service of the town. Curiously, *A Man to Remember* was a remake after only a five-year lapse of a Lionel Barrymore film, *One Man's Journey*, which had been scripted by a writer also to become one of the "Hollywood Ten," Samuel Ornitz.

*A Man to Remember* was a critical rather than a commercial success, however, and Trumbo found few other chances to shame the screen audience with evidence of its indifference to those it should have honored. He was usually kept busy with such projects as an attempt to write, with Ernest Pagano, a film script that would capitalize upon the attention the public was showering on "Flying Irishman" Douglas Corrigan, who had made a "wrong-way" flight across the Atlantic. Perhaps not coincidentally, Trumbo was promoted from routine "B" films to the more ambitious "A's," upon which the prestige of the industry rested, just after he enjoyed some literary acclaim for his third novel, *Johnny Got His Gun.*

It would be difficult to challenge the right of this novel to the American Booksellers' Award as the "most original" novel of 1939—or almost any year. The sickening tale of a "basket case's" struggle to re-establish communication with the rest of humanity demonstrates its author's extraordinary imaginative power. The pacifist plea embodied in this grim narrative might also have made the novel one of the most influential of the decade if it had appeared only a year earlier, about the time that Neville Chamberlain returned from Munich holding out the pathetically awaited hope for "peace in our time." Trumbo, however, had trouble timing the appearance of his novels. By the time *Johnny Got His Gun* appeared in—of all the inappropriate months—September, 1939, not only Spain and Czechoslovakia had fallen, but Poland, too; and though Americans still strove desperately to avoid war, their efforts were already appearing doomed.

*Johnny Got His Gun* was more, however, than an angry and haunting cry for peace; like Trumbo's earlier works it was actually a denunciation of all organized society, much more nearly anarchist than anything else in its philosophy, even though it was serialized in the Communist sponsored *Daily Worker.* It remains emotionally gripping today. Always a competent craftsman, Trumbo carefully manipulated his effects to produce the most agonized response in those readers with stomachs strong enough to stick to the tale at all.

The first part is a protracted account, interrupted by frequent flashbacks into the carefree past, of soldier Joe Bonham's discovery that he is deaf and blind, that he has lost all four limbs and all of his face below his forehead, and that he has an incurable running wound in his side. In the second part of the story, this seemingly hopelessly isolated blob of flesh, after an incredibly long and painful struggle, learns to communicate with the world again by Morse code. His efforts, however, prove unavailing when he is peremptorily informed that his request to be put on exhibition as a warning to others of the horrors of war is "against regulations." [11] Since as Joe sees it, "he was a perfect picture of the future" and the authorities are "afraid to let anyone see what the future was like," [12] he is put under opiates to still his restlessness.

As reviewers acknowledged when the book appeared, the shock of the story is unforgettable. Trumbo undoubtedly counted upon its effect being powerful enough to inhibit close analysis of his technique, for such examination raises misgivings about the humanitarianism of the motives that prompted the tale. *Johnny Got His Gun* is not, like *The Grapes of Wrath*, a cautionary tale, pleading urgently for reform before it is too late—a tale directed to those in a position to effect the reforms. Rather it is a revolutionary tract calling upon the modern slave—as Joe identifies himself—to rise against his oppressors before he is reduced to Joe's helpless state. Even the account, through Joe's stream-of-consciousness, of his condition is interrupted by a long condemnation of those "who are willing to sacrifice somebody else's life," and in the last paragraph as Joe sinks into narcotic delirium, the stream of his consciousness bears an inflammatory message for the little people of the world.

> We are men of peace we are men who work and we want no quarrel. But if you destroy our peace if you take away our work if you try to range us one against the other we will know what to do. If you tell us to make the world safe for democracy we will take you seriously and by god and by Christ we will make it so. We will use the guns you force upon us we will use them to defend our very lives and the menace to our lives does not lie on the other side of a

nomansland that was set apart without our consent it lies within our own boundaries here and now we have seen it and we know it.[13]

The tract, although looked down upon, is a perfectly legitimate literary form. One may object, however, to discrepancies between the author's professed aim and his manipulation of his materials. Careful scrutiny of Trumbo's novel leads one to question whether it was really prompted by outraged sympathy for those sufferers symbolized by Joe Bonham. Since Joe would not be able to communicate whatever message he has to the world, the only assurance the reader has of the nature of the gospel of this "new kind of Christ" comes through Trumbo's serving as his interpreter.[14]

It is enlightening to contrast the ending of this novel with that of Steinbeck's *In Dubious Battle* (1936), which it quite literally parallels, for in Steinbeck's book an agitator hauls the dead and *faceless* body of a former colleague before a susceptible crowd. I have explained the symbolism of this action in an earlier analysis of the novel.

> The organizers are just as much exploiters as the growers [against whom the strike is directed]. The case against them is summarized in the savagely ironic symbol of Jim's faceless body at the end of the book. Mac brings the body back to a meeting of the strikers and places a lantern "carefully on the floor, so that its light [falls] on the head." This gesture makes explicit Steinbeck's objection to the exploiters of human dignity.[15]

In writing his novel, Trumbo did precisely what Mac, the organizer in the Steinbeck novel, does—focus a lantern on a shattered face and body so that he can exploit it in presenting his own revolutionary message. Trumbo employed precisely the tactics that Steinbeck had castigated three years earlier.

Although reviewers were generally horrified by the details of Joe's condition, they admired the author's imaginative brilliance. Only the reviewer for the *Atlantic Monthly* suggested that it was "philosophically not quite fair." [16] *Johnny Got His Gun* also sold well enough to have gone through eight printings by the end of 1946; but despite the booksellers' award, the novel did not attract either the critical attention or sales that its novelty and power seemed to warrant. Trumbo's acrimoniousness was probably already making people uneasy. The next year he encountered his only recorded trouble with Hollywood producers over a script.

He was responsible for both the original story and the screenplay of *We Who Are Young.* Dorothy B. Jones reports in "Communism and the Movies," a study of the content of films with which the "Hollywood Ten" were associated, that the first version of this work contained material identifiable as Communist propaganda and that Trumbo had to revise the story twice before Metro-Goldwyn-Mayer would buy it. Even then he "was put to work under the direction of the producer, to revise the story along lines which the studio wished it to follow." [17] Despite all this effort, the tale of an unemployed young couple struggling in New York was dismissed by *New York Times* reviewer Bosley Crowther as "slow and drab" [18] and was ignored by most serious film critics. Trumbo's desire to propagandize seems to have won out over his art; certainly his last novel, *The Remarkable Andrew*, would have been little more than another heart-rending tale of frustrated youth miraculously vindicated, if it had not been for the interpolated diatribes.

By the time this novel appeared, Trumbo, who had also fashioned a screenplay from Christopher Morley's best-selling novel *Kitty Foyle*, had a large enough reputation to receive serious treatment in almost every important periodical. Most reviewers praised the imaginative quality of Trumbo's fantasy about an honest young bookkeeper rescued from scheming superiors by the ghost of Andrew

Jackson, who rallies the shades of Washington, Jefferson, Franklin, Marshall, and Jesse James to plot the youth's defense. Had this been all there was to this tale of an out-of-step young man who tried to embody Trumbo's concept of Jacksonian principles in the corrupt modern world, it might have slipped by unnoticed in a country now preoccupied with the war that Trumbo had pleaded be avoided.

The patriotic fantasy, however, simply provides a framework for a virulent attack on America's alliance with England, which closely follows the Communist line of the time.[19] Reactions to the book varied with the isolationist or interventionist inclinations of the reviewer. Holmes Alexander found it "likeable" and "important," [20] but Beatrice Sherman in the *New York Times* described "its blending of the didactic and fantastic, the romantic and practical" as "more remarkable than felicitous." [21] As one might have expected, the novel was most vigorously condemned by the London *Times Literary Supplement*.

> the lengthy couple of chapters in the middle in which General Andrew Jackson roaringly lets himself go in support of the extreme isolationist point of view in the United States to-day leave a nasty taste in the mouth. The misrepresentation that apparently feeds such suicidal tendencies in the matter as exist in America in 1941 is anything but a joke.[22]

Again Trumbo's timing was unfortunate. By the time his book was released even the Communists were ready to abandon isolationism, as they did when Germany attacked Russia just three months after *The Remarkable Andrew* was published. Perhaps Trumbo's inability to keep his propaganda in step with the march of events at least partially explains his confining his literary efforts after the appearance of *The Remarkable Andrew* to scriptwriting, and one tasteless attempt in *The Biggest Thief in Town* (1949) to combine comedy and propaganda in a Broadway play.

Trumbo has no claim to recognition as a successful artist in traditional media; yet he cannot be dismissed from literary studies, because few men tried harder during the years immediately preceding America's entry into World War II to write what I have defined as social novels, works dealing with the individual's relationship to specific social situations of his time. He tried to depict the plight of the individual confronted by the depression, expanding bureaucracy, the drift toward war, and official corruption. Since these were serious problems, some examination of the reasons for Trumbo's failure to handle them impressively sheds light on the particular problems facing the artist who attempts to write this kind of novel.

The conspicuous difference between Trumbo's novels and the three around which this study is built, lies in the motivating philosophies of the authors. Faulkner, Hemingway, and Steinbeck all believed that the only real hope for the future resided in the individual who continued to fight for the things that he believed in. Even if the particular individual were destroyed in his effort to preserve his integrity, these authors did not believe that his spirit could be quenched by the forces that sought to destroy him. All three, although not necessarily directly influenced by Emerson, reflected the transcendentalist's doctrine of "self-reliance" and his belief that in the longest view evil would prove transitory.

Trumbo's work, on the other hand, consistently embodied the cynical and pessimistic philosophy that the individual could not defeat the system, but was doomed to be crushed by it. As the ghastly remnant of Joe Bonham reflects in *Johnny Got His Gun*, "This thing wasn't any of your business. What do you care about making the world safe for democracy? . . . Yet here you are and it was none of your affair." [23] At the end of Trumbo's first three novels, John Abbott, Henry Hogg, and Joe Bonham are all cruelly and completely annihilated by an ungrateful society that fails to recognize their claims upon it. While young Andrew Long does at last triumph in *The Remarkable Andrew,* he does so only with fantastic assistance, so that the novel has no relation to the problems of living in modern society. Even in this novel Trumbo finds a defense for those who framed Andrew: he feels that they, too, "had been cheated by their environment, betrayed by their gods, and so they had grown cynical and rapacious. . . . But they were not soundly evil." [24] He could never bear to face the solemn consequences of making man responsible for himself.

Trumbo's point of view that the individual cannot transcend his environment is summarized in one of the last lines of his play, *The Biggest Thief in Town,* "It's either steal or go broke." [25] At the end of *Eclipse,* Trumbo pays passing tribute to the old woman who lives unassumingly by the river, but there is no evidence elsewhere in his work that he really cared for the unassuming person. He consistently implied, on the other hand, that particular individuals were important in themselves rather than for what they represented. Indeed his first three protagonists do not seem really to represent anything at all except a strong yearning for personal success, and it is doubtful if all who fancied themselves subscribers to Jacksonian principles could have recognized themselves in the prissy and humorless Andrew Long. Trumbo's novels were actually glorifications of the very individual ego that Steinbeck's Joads at long last learned to control, that Hemingway's characters find brings only loneliness and isolation, and that Faulkner castigates through his portrayal of Flem Snopes.

Trumbo's preoccupation with the egotistical individual is not enough in itself, however, to explain the weakness of his novels, for other authors like Thomas Wolfe have been able to forge enduring artistic monuments from the apotheosis of the individual ego. Trumbo's fundamental failure was his inability to fuse his clever but contrived stories with the doctrines wordily propounded by his characters. He was most successful in involved, but lightweight tales like his early short stories and movie scripts; his novels would have been better with the rant removed, although they would then hardly have been more than superficial exploitations of the social scene.

The difference between the hack writer and the serious artist lies principally in the latter's having, besides the former's skill in mechanically constructing a story (and some exceptional artists like Emily Brontë lack that), a vision of life that he dramatizes through his story. In eminently successful works like Steinbeck's "The Red Pony" or Faulkner's "The Bear" or Hemingway's "Big, Two-Hearted River," this underlying vision is completely presented through the unfolding of the story itself, so that the plot and theme, to use helpful traditional terms, are completely and inseparably fused. If the artist is unable to achieve this fusion, the work divides—as all Trumbo's novels do—into two unresolved segments. Such failure may result either from the writer's inability to devise a plot that can successfully embody his ideas or—more likely—from a conflict that he does not perceive between the point that he wants the reader to get from the story and the point that the story actually makes.

Since the ability to perceive and eliminate such discrepancies requires the most rigid kind of dispassionate self-analysis, whereas the creation of a moving and memorable story requires such highly subjective attributes as a vivid imagination and great emotional warmth, these abilities are rarely combined in one individual. What we can learn from the consideration of the works of a writer like Dalton Trumbo is that the wonder is, not that great and enduring social novels are rare, but that they exist at all in view of the unlikely amalgam their creation demands. Trumbo's inability to be a tough enough judge of either his characters or himself as an artist, provides us with a perspective by which we achieve some concept of the extraordinary qualities of writers like Faulkner, Steinbeck, and Hemingway that we often fail to recognize when, considering them in isolation, we focus attention on their shortcomings.

## ii

By one of those eerie coincidences that enliven the study of literature as outside the realm of statistical probability, the shamefully neglected novel that provides the best epitaph for the tarnished age of modern Imperialism was published just the week before World War II broke out.

*Ararat* was not entirely ignored when it appeared. Although most reviewers were confused by its failure to conform to superficial formulae that they wished to impose upon it, the most sensitive, Stephen Vincent Benét, hailed the novel handsomely, and when the next awards season rolled around, *Ararat* was honored both by the Friends of American Literature as the best book by a midwesterner and by the American Booksellers' Association as its "discovery" of the year. Since then, however, this complex and disturbing novel has received little critical attention, although its story and its theme both have a universal significance that entitles it to attention as one of those rare works that illuminate persisting patterns of human behavior at the same time that they portray the troubled history of a particular time and place.

About the only similarities between Dalton Trumbo and Elgin Groseclose, the Oklahoma-born author of *Ararat*, are that both come from the arid regions of the American West, both achieved their principal reputations for works other than their fiction, and both were violently critical of those who used public office for private gain. Their wrath, however, found vastly different outlets. Whereas Trumbo preached an extreme isolationism verging on anarchy and leading to the unqualified exaltation of the individual ego, Groseclose argued for the conquest of this ego and the development of a self-absorbing responsibility for all mankind based on the fundamental Christian concept of placing one's trust in God rather than in human "causes" or systems. He became, therefore, at a time when religious fiction seemed the exclusive preserve of slick and sentimental soul-savers, preaching "pie in the sky," a writer who attempted to restore to unabashedly religious works some of the austere and soul-shaking drama of the prophets. Clifton Fadiman was not jesting when he later described Groseclose as "Lloyd Douglas without *Schmalz*," [26] but the public craved *schmalz*, and the neglect of *Ararat* exposes the superficiality of those who periodically call for a return to religion in serious fiction.

Groseclose is most distinguished, not as a churchman, however, but as an authority on monetary systems and a financial advisor to the American and Iranian governments. This international authority on money was born in, of all unlikely places, Waukomis, in north-central Oklahoma, center of the Dust Bowl in the thirties. He was born in 1899, just six years after his father had claimed a homestead during the famous land rush at the opening of the Cherokee Strip. The wild country of his youth exercised comparatively little influence, however, on his writings, which were inspired rather by the two years that he spent—following his graduation in 1920 from the University of Oklahoma—in Tabriz, Persia, where he taught in a Presbyterian missionary high school and served as secretary to the Persian Committee on Near East Relief.

His work for this group brought him into the starving republics that had been set up in the Caucasus. Following the collapse of the Imperial Russian government, Armenia, Azerbaijan, and Georgia had declared their independence and sought relief and military assistance from Russia's former allies. The inefficiency of the new governments, the inadequacy of relief efforts, and the aggressive designs of both the new Turkish Republic and the Soviet Union quickly doomed these fledgling states. Before their fall Groseclose had, however, had a chance to work at the "City of Children," an Alexandropol orphanage where 25,000 homeless waifs were cared for in former army barracks by the Near Eastern relief committee. His experiences there provided the setting for the climactic scenes in *Ararat* as well as his detailed knowledge of the tragic history of the pathetic remnants of the ancient Armenian people. After the Caucasian republics were reabsorbed into Russia, the American relief commission was regarded with extreme suspicion. When Groseclose tried to depart through customs at the port of Batum, his life-insurance policy number was interpreted as a police number, and he was held prisoner for a month, on charges of espionage, by the Cheka (Commission Extraordinary for the Suppression of Counter-Revolutionary Propaganda),[27] whose activities he bitterly indicts in *Ararat*.

His missionary zeal apparently cooled by his ordeal, Groseclose returned to his financial studies at American University in Washington, D. C., where he received master's and doctor's degrees. He also served during the twenties as financial specialist in the Department of Commerce, and in 1928 he moved to one of the large banks in New York City. From December, 1930, to March, 1932, his name appeared on the masthead of the lush new business journal *Fortune* as an associate editor, and during the same period he taught at the City College of New York. The next academic year, however, found him back at the University of Oklahoma, as as assistant professor of business English, a post that he retained until 1938, although during his last years of service to his native state he began also to work as an investigator for the federal government.

In the late twenties Groseclose had published several specialized monographs on Asiatic finances, but during his years back home, he began to write for a popular audience. His first book for the general public, *Money: The Human Conflict* (1934), resulted from a suggestion by the editor of the University of Oklahoma Press that Groseclose prepare "a work that would explain in simple terms the devaluation of the dollar that had just occurred and the events that made this devaluation necessary." [28] This work, not only relates briefly and fascinatingly the history of man's frustrating experiences with money, but also sets forth the ethical concepts that underlie the author's novels, the first of which, *The Persian Journey of the Reverend Ashley Wishard and His Servant Fathi* (1937), dates from his years of teaching in Oklahoma.

Although it suffers from many defects common to first novels, *The Persian Journey* is important as a preliminary announcement of the themes that were to motivate its author's most ambitious work. The early novel is a kind of spiritual picaresque which relates the Reverend Wishard's gradual discovery of his own purpose in life as his travels through remote and bandit-ridden regions of Persia carry him steadily further from the aggressive, machine-minded civilization that produced him. The trouble with the novel is that, as the *New Yorker* put it, it is a "combination of travelogue and sermon" rather than a work of fiction. Intent upon clarifying the serious theme that prompted him to write, Groseclose fails to dramatize his points and instead simply alternates bits of local color with reports of the Reverend Wishard's soul struggles.

The work suffers even from a lack of consistent tone. The introductory account of Wishard's ludicrous difficulties with modern transportation in Persia, and of his sponsoring Church of the Age's role in dispensing religion to upper Park Avenue, make the book at first seem like an early satirization, with a gospel flavoring, of the obtuse and bumbling American abroad that has become a familiar figure in post-World War II literature. Satirical jibes like that about Wishard's leaving America "when there was so much missionary cultivation needed there," [29] soon are left behind, however, and the later chapters tell a story closely akin to that of William Faulkner's "The Bear," about the way in which a civilized man can share the primitive world only if he strips himself of the corrupting accouterments of his civilization. Wishard learns this lesson when he begins "to see in the machine, and in the machine-dominated civilization, the antithesis of all Christianity." [30]

The change in tone is probably designed to underline Wishard's own conversion from a dynamic evangelist to a passive believer. At the beginning of his mission, he has supposed that "the task of the Christian evangelist" is to awaken "the spark of divinity in the hearts of men, the consciousness that man is more than the puppet of fate," [31] but after he at last wins acceptance from the tough and suspicious Kurds, he embraces a new concept.

> And so when his listeners questioned him about this Christ of his, and of the meaning of the Christian message, Ashley no longer resorted to the concept of the Promethean man, the man who was conquering his physical world by the sword of the spirit. He told them rather of the Christian man, who was conquering self by the power of love, and finding God through Christ.[32]

Groseclose strains so hard to make his point, however, that he seems to be discovering it in the course of composing the narrative, just as his character is discovering his purpose as he journeys. Readers, however, expect an author before publishing to have resolved the confusions that trouble his character. *The Persian Journey*'s principal interest today is in the startling contrast it affords with its author's skillful dramatic embodiment only two and a half years later in *Ararat* of the theme he handles clumsily here.

At first glance *Ararat* does not appear to be a social novel in the restricted definition of the term that I am employing. It utilizes as its background the tragic efforts—too little known to Americans—of the Armenians of the late nineteenth and early twentieth centuries to re-establish themselves as an independent nation. The principal character is an American missionary who has chosen to make the relief of the Armenians his life's work; and because of the author's preoccupation with ideological conflicts, the novel has usually been vaguely classified as "philosophical."

Yet it has as a great social significance as any other novel of its period. The events that it describes occurred between 1895 and 1922, entirely within the era that closed with the fall of Paris; the period covered is, in fact, almost identical with that of the events reflected in Faulkner's *The Hamlet*. The disorders in Turkey and Russia that Groseclose depicts were instrumental in leading to both World Wars, and the author was acutely aware that the Turkish persecutions of Armenians directly paralleled the more publicized treatment of larger minorities in Europe in the thirties. The aggressive Turkish and Russian leaders are clearly akin in philosophy and policy to the totalitarians of the thirties, and the author writes of the region and its troubles not with the secondhand knowledge of the historical novelist, but from the viewpoint of a spectator who had observed, studied, and even suffered at the hands of those whom he depicts. *Ararat* portrays a foreshadowing of the tendencies that ran rampant in the thirties and renders almost unbearably graphic in an artistically constructed work the consequences of these tendencies.

The artistic merit of the novel was not apparent to its first reviewers, who, considering the book a recounting of Armenian attempts to shake off Russian and Turkish rule, objected to the episodic construction. What only Stephen Vincent Benét recognized at the time was that the novel was not actually "historical" at all and that the episodes in which the American missionary became involved were not just selected scenes in a frustrated campaign for freedom.

The novel is, rather, a gripping dramatization of the dialectic process by which Groseclose arrived at his conclusion that, as Benét puts it, "Pure goodness is likely to be martyred, pure will to break itself against a wall. But when goodness and will combine there is hope for the race." [33] The novel makes great demands on the reader because, in order to grasp the author's point, one must keep all of the seemingly disparate fragments in mind until all are interrelated and the multiple strands of the plot are resolved in the breathtaking final pages as an army of children is delivered, like the ancient Hebrews fleeing Egypt, out of the hands of the oppressor.

This rescue is effected by the combined efforts of characters whose hitherto separate histories disturbed reviewers seeking an orderly, cumulative chain of events leading to a logical climax. One discovers the underlying purpose of *Ararat,* however, not by outlining the plot, but by studying the method by which the characters are brought together. The first principal introduced is Amos Lyle, a former Texas cowboy turned missionary, who by leading the remnants of an Armenian community to an unstable refuge in late nineteenth-century Russia saves this community from the Turkish overlords who seek to decimate it. In Russia, however, he is obliged to witness the community, which was never warmly welcomed, gradually deteriorate and disperse. When at last after World War I Armenia achieves a short-lived independence, he finds new usefulness as the founder of a "city of children" like that Groseclose visited.

Lyle is assisted in his efforts by Sarani, the comely Armenian daughter of victims of the Turkish purge, whom he adopts, and also, quite unexpectedly, by the vigorous chief of a band of nomads that rove the northwestern wastes of Persia, who had been one of Lyle's first followers in the early days of his mission.

The necessary executive talent for the migration of the children to Persia when their orphanage is threatened with

destruction by resurgent Turks is provided by Paul Stepan-
ovitch Markov, sole survivor of a Russian military family,
who has himself twice been nearly killed by fanatical
revolutionaries after the collapse of the old regime. Out-
cast from his homeland, Markov is offered a commission in
the new Armenian army; but when he accidentally becomes acquainted with Lyle, who knew Markov's father,
he rejects the Army and labors to preserve the orphans in
whom he sees the only hope for the future. Markov's
conversion to the works of peace is not, however, simply an
inexplicable fictional convenience or an inscrutable act of
providence, for from the beginning the young man has
been distinguished from his dying class by his recognition
that he gets the best results from his men, not by following
military school theories but by dealing with the troops "as
human beings, as persons like himself." [34]

Groseclose might have made his work tighter and more
easily comprehensible if he had used the familiar device of
the flashback, begun with the evacuation of the children
across a raging river to Persia, and disclosed the histories of
his characters in relationship to this event; but his purpose
would not have been served by such a slick and easily read
tale. By presenting a rapid succession of compressed
vignettes, he forces the reader to share with the characters
the protracted development of the sorrows and uncertain-
ties that are resolved in the final redemption of the
children.

That the novel is far from an artless work is demonstrated by the author's handling of two nearly parallel
"miracles," the salvation by a snowstorm that frustrates
Turkish pursuit of the band of Armenians fleeing to
Russia in the 1890's, and the salvation by a flash flood
that cuts off the pursuers, more than a quarter of a century
later, of the children fleeing to Persia. Rather than extract
the full dramatic possibilities from the first episode, which
follows hard on the heels of a sickening account of the
massacre of defenseless men, Groseclose has it reported

only briefly and at second hand, so that the impact of the novel's finale will not be destroyed by the event that foreshadows it.

Nor does Groseclose yield to the temptation to capitalize upon the recurrent sensational episodes in the necessarily bloody story of the violence attendant upon irresponsible ambition, because he is primarily interested in looking through events at the forces that motivated them. His attack is directed primarily, however, not at the kind of subconscious forces that turn once ardent humanitarians into sadistic monsters, but at the perversions of logic that provide the antihumanitarians with grotesque rationalizations. In one of the most chilling of the passages, a former kindly humanist whom a taste of violence and power has turned bloodthirsty, is explaining to a group of prisoners why they must be liquidated; this man, Belinsky, offers the argument that might persuade otherwise inoffensive people to tolerate totalitarian programs of extermination.

"After full deliberation a decision has been made. It is a decision with which you will agree. You can well realize the danger to the State, and the inconvenience and unhappiness to yourselves, if you were released. First, you have no friends. Second, you have no homes. Third, you have no place in the new society. The order into which you were born has vanished; the society which you knew is broken and dispersed. The ideals which you upheld have dissolved into a new ideal which you do not recognize. There is no place for you here, no security, no refuge. All that lies ahead. You will find peace and refuge and your friends, but you will find them ahead, not behind you.

"Nor would you wish to return, should there be here and there a stray friend. What would be the result? You might struggle bravely. But why struggle when it is hopeless? A new order has already been fixed for a new generation. Would you again stir up strife among the people you love, and disrupt the order and well-being of our country by renewed civil war? You would not. The Soviet State answers for you." (pp. 281–82)

Groseclose considers the principal villain to be, however, the destructive philosophies embraced by late nineteenth-century European intellectuals in place of a constructive faith. He first describes the thinking that he challenges in his portrait of an ambitious Turk, Hashim Farouk Bey, who is responsible for both efforts to wipe out the Armenian communities.

> He had attended scientific and philosophical lectures and had learned, at secondhand, of the great philosophers of Europe—Descartes, Leibnitz, Hegel, Spinoza, and Hobbes —and of the lesser ones, Schopenhauer and Nietzsche, who were setting mankind aright as to what men should believe concerning God and man and morals.
>
> .  .  .  .  .  .  .  .  .  .  .  .  .  .  .
>
> Hashim Farouk Bey had acquired some positive disbeliefs from the lectures on philosophy, but as for any positive beliefs—the philosophers had been most confusing. To Descartes, for instance, God was the Prime Mover of prime matter. This was explained to mean that the universe was a machine—a machine that worked automatically in accordance with foreordained law, in which there was no compassion, no hope, no love. Leibnitz had expressed it more clearly—"The Universe is a clockwork of God."
>
> .  .  .  .  .  .  .  .  .  .  .  .  .  .  .
>
> Hashim Farouk Bey had found nourishment in the pessimism of Schopenhauer and in the masterful, vigorous concepts of Nietzsche. From them he had learned, as a matter of dogma, that there was no pity, nor softness, nor remorse, nor love in the mechanism of the universe: it operated by law and logic and force—beautifully or fantastically or horribly, as one saw it—but with that same contempt for human hopes or desires or fears as a locomotive on a track or the great looms and spinning wheels in the cotton factories of Manchester. (pp. 76–77)

Groseclose thus joins those who put the blame for the collapse of an irresponsible age on the increasing automatism of its intellectuals—a mindless mechanization, which coupled with "the ferment of nationalism" sweeping all Europe at the time, made "regard for humanity . . . only mawkish sentiment." The rest of the novel is unified by the author's arguments against the consideration of man as merely a logical mechanism, as he felt this idea led to the theory that minorities "should be dealt with in a purely scientific fashion, that is, simply as chemical elements of an amalgam that were to be burned out with fire" (p. 78).

In contrast to Hashim Farouk Bey, Groseclose poses Amos Lyle, who rejects the logical contemplation of men as either "chemical and physical combinations of elements to form bone, tissue, and brain cells, together with a mental switchboard that operates by impulses, either environmental or hereditary" or as simply units of a precisely organized state, because to Lyle

> man was a thing of infinite capacity, of infinite worth, a creature made in the image of God, and a partaker of divinity through Jesus Christ, a creature upon whom no bounds were set, for whom law had ceased to be—as St. Paul had said—and who was possessed of matchless freedom in the Lord. (p. 104)

Lyle does not, however, undermine the integrity of his convictions and fall into the trap that single-minded zealots do by attempting to use logic to refute the logic of foes whose mastery of the art they concede. Even to his Armenian friends, who argue passionately for independence on logical grounds, Lyle replies, "What you say is very logical and appealing . . . and I will not attempt to answer with logic, remembering that the gospel was foolishness to the Greeks, greatest masters of all of the logical processes" (p. 159). Lyle sidesteps the pit into which wishful thinking plummeted so many nobly disposed persons of the early twentieth century who supposed that an unswerving adherence to the principle of self-determination might by itself prove a political panacea, for he recognized when he coupled what is logical with what is appealing that the proponents of logic might be committed to the methods of logic only so long as they served their preconceptions. Logic is too austere a faith to attract many unswayable disciples. Lyle's thoughts about the insufficiency of logic were probably inspired by Groseclose's observations of the ill-fated Caucasian Republics of the twenties.

> The imposition of democratic institutions did not necessarily make for democracy. . . . Nor, on the other hand, would the denial, or destruction, of democratic institutions destroy the spirit of democracy among peoples who had known its blessings. Democracy could live without institutions, but the institutions were sterile without the spirit. (p. 162)

He maintains his faith, too, against the arguments of Paul Markov, who until he meets Lyle has lived by logic. When Markov argues that they should not rely simply upon chance to feed and care for the many children in the orphanage, Lyle replies without condescension:

> "I realize that it is hard for those who have been brought up in a world of logic, dominated by the law of cause and effect, to realize the meaning of chance in the ways of God. . . . But I have found them to occur so often and with such regularity as to have no doubt of God's merciful and constant provision for His creatures. Perhaps, in certain fields of human activity, men must rely upon the laws of certainty, but in others, where the laws of certainty have broken down, reliance must be upon the Author of law, rather than upon the law." (p. 325)

These arguments quoted out of context oversimplify the novel, for they make it appear that Lyle is the author's spokesman and that the author is arguing for a blind faith in providence as the only directing force in human affairs; but Groseclose is too sophisticated to offer such simple Sunday school morality as Clifton Fadiman supposed he did, describing the novel as "a prosy sermon on the superiority of primitive Christianity to the Nietzschean doctrines of will and force." [35] Amos Lyle does not ultimately save his people singlehanded like an ecclesiastical Lone Ranger. Despite what Lyle says, faith is not presented in this novel as an adequate remedy in itself for the world's ills. Lyle is not taking as irresponsible a position as those he condemns by advocating implicit trust in special providences. The first community that Lyle founds in Russia disintegrates, and it is necessary for others, like Markov, to devise the plans that make it possible to save the children of Lyle's second community.

The saint is not necessarily a good administrator. Lyle is inefficient, largely ineffective, in making converts, and often careless about obligations he assumes. Groseclose's point is, not that the faithful can save the world, single-handed, but that except for Lyle's inspiration, the abilities and energies of others, like Markov, would have been directed toward destruction rather than creation. Markov originally had an arrogant aristocratic faith in "the sufficiency of . . . the individual will," but he perceived the limitations of this philosophy when he saw it being used with effectiveness equal to that of the defenders of his society, to vindicate the policies of his Red opponents. He thus comes to recognize that if he rejects the Revolution, he "must reject the intellectual propositions which he had come unquestioningly to accept" (p. 260).

As Stephen Vincent Benét's review points out, Groseclose maintains that "goodness and will" must combine if there is to be any hope for the race. The quality that Lyle brings into human affairs is perhaps best explained by his adopted daughter, who through her marriage to Markov brings about the fusion of the best representatives of the two forces. When Markov, still addicted to the logic instilled in him by his military training, argues for "absolute justice, . . . absolute equality of treatment" in handling the children, Sarani replies, "That may be for grown-ups—soldiers, possibly—but not for children. . . . They do not have a mathematical sense, and their spirit of

generosity is more developed than their sense of justice.
What gives joy to one gives, by reflection, joy to all" (p.
360). The meaning of Sarani's words comes home finally
to Markov when the driving force of his will is satisfied at
last by his individual physical conquest of the towering
peak of Ararat. Then, at peace with himself, he discovers
that his faith is re-invigorated by the delivery of the
children from their persecutors.

> His pity went out toward all men, toward all those children
> of God who still struggled against life, against each other, in
> hatred and arrogance, destroying themselves, and destroy-
> ing the beauty and harmony which God so much desired
> for them. . . . Here, he thought, was the secret of the
> mystery and the ineffable mystery itself. In love were the
> Will of God and the will of man united, in love was the
> understanding from which all harmony proceeds, and in
> love was the sanctuary and salvation which all men desire.
> (pp. 480–82)

Finally, within a more traditionally orthodox framework
than the other writers of his period, Groseclose arrived at
precisely the same conclusion as Hemingway, Faulkner,
and Steinbeck, that the solutions to the world's ills could
not be found in causes, parties, and States, but only in the
unique individual's learning at last through his own tribu-
lations that the only hope for the future lay in his own
acceptance as an isolated being of a conscious and self-
sacrificing responsibility for the whole of mankind.

Groseclose conspicuously and necessarily refuses to identify Christianity with any particular church, or even to set
it apart from Islam, the other religion he knew from
firsthand experience. His fictional sermon preaches not the
glory of a sect, but the individual acceptance of God as a
creative force. His book does not, in fact, preach that
Christianity is the sole road to the world's salvation, but
rather that it still does offer a road to peace—and a better
road than some proposed alternatives. The snow-covered

peak of Ararat, where according to Biblical tradition the patriarch who had individually accepted God learned that man was to have a second chance, towers significantly above the novel as both ancient symbol and present reality. To an age that the novelist felt had destroyed itself by coupling ruthless will with joyless logic, he offered, too, the hope of rebirth through the co-operation rather than the implacable opposition of the inspired traditionalist and the dynamic intellectual.

Since the publication of *Ararat*, Groseclose has written several other novels—*The Firedrake* (1942), *The Carmelite* (1955), and a children's tale *The Scimitar of Saladin* (1950)—but all are based on episodes in nineteenth-century New England and still older Persian history and cannot by any extension of the term be considered social novels. He has also continued to distinguish himself as an economist.[36] In January, 1943, he returned to Persia with an American economic mission that hoped to control runaway inflation in that country during its wartime occupation by Allied forces. Groseclose served for some months as Treasurer General and helped curb inflation by the public sale of gold; but feeling that in view of the policies of the mission's head, he could render no efficient service, he resigned after six months [37] and returned to Washington as an economic counsellor to corporations and the federal government. He has also served as Director of the Institute for Monetary Research and the International Council for Christian Leadership.

His writing has received scant recognition in literary chronicles, but *Ararat* deserves renewed attention as a skillful work of art. It presents the theme of the necessity for individual effort to regenerate the world that dominated the most distinguished social fiction of its period; it presents this theme against the broadest geographical and ideological background that any of the novelists employed.

THE STRIKING THING about the three monumental novels
that Faulkner, Hemingway, and Steinbeck produced at the
end of the age of irresponsibility is the underlying similarities of viewpoint expressed by the three novelists whose
dissimilarities have been most frequently noticed. *The
Hamlet, For Whom the Bell Tolls,* and *The Grapes of
Wrath* are all grounded in the same long American literary
tradition of individualism. All three of them expound
through Ratliff, Robert Jordan, and Tom Joad some version of the doctrine of self-reliance that distinguished the
works of Emerson, Thoreau, and Whitman as among the
first efforts to forge a distinctly American ideology.

Steinbeck's relationship to the transcendentalists was
pointed out soon after *The Grapes of Wrath* appeared by
Frederic I. Carpenter,[1] and as the thirties fade into history,
Jim Casy with his idea of the holiness of all men and the
unreality of sin seems less a product of his own narrowly
doctrinaire age than a latter-day wanderer from the green
village of Concord to the dry plains of the West. Although
Steinbeck argues for collective action to achieve specific
goals, only the most unperceptive critics continue to argue
that he is a collectivist in either philosophy or politics.
Throughout his work he decries the mindless indoctrina-
tion of the totalitarians and maintains that only the
individual through reflection upon his bitter experience

can learn the value of acting in concert with others for the relief of emergency conditions—like the flood at the end of *The Grapes of Wrath*—so that the individual may subsequently be free to realize his own potentialities. Nothing better illustrates Steinbeck's concept of social organization than the picture in Chapter Seventeen of *The Grapes of Wrath* of the world that is created each night as people come together, and disappears the next morning when they separate.

In Hemingway's hands the concept of individualism is distorted into an almost grotesque rejection of the enduring value of human associations. Almost all of Hemingway's principal characters, from *The Sun Also Rises* to *The Old Man and the Sea*, end up like Harry Morgan and Robert Jordan utterly alone, surrounded by marine or human sharks, awaiting the oblivion that will end their pain. Some, like Nick in "Big, Two-Hearted River," admit that they are happiest by themselves, and others, like Frederic Henry, seem happier alone than they are willing to admit. Although by comparison with Henry Miller and his disciples, Hemingway seems a decorous writer, he is really the father of the cult of the orgasm, for he appears to be able to conceive of meaningful relationships between individuals only in terms of fleeting, physical, emotion-choked contacts. All of his characters share the ability, that reaches its apogee in Robert Jordan, to separate their public life as a lone operator from their private life as an ardent lover. Hemingway is less able than Faulkner or even Steinbeck to force his characters to face social reality; and he remains essentially a writer of escape fiction, even though his manly characters are obliged to suffer through tough escapes rather than ride tenderly into the sunset as in the more conventional forms of twentieth-century romanticism.

Faulkner's novel, which is gradually winning deserved recognition as the most complicated and uncompromising of the three, contrasts through the portraits of Flem Snopes and Ratliff, two forms of individualism in order to suggest that individualism in itself is not necessarily a merit. Often it has been objected that the kind of self-reliance Emerson preaches could indeed lead to the inhuman excesses of fascism if the individual insists on gratifying his private whims without regard to the rights of others. In his portrayal of Flem Snopes (and many other characters in his novels), Faulkner presents the ultimate embodiment of the Nietzschean superman as a Mississippi redneck, destroying whatever stands in the path of his own aggrandizement. But the evils of Snopesism do not lead Faulkner to denounce individualism, for Ratliff, too, is an individualist with a primary concern for his private interests, but yet moved by the desire to protect "something that . . . wouldn't know how to hurt no man even if it would and wouldn't want to even if it could." This quality—the love that Elgin Groseclose maintains must for success be paired with will—distinguishes Ratliff from the Snopeses, who do not find a constructive gratification in doing their own jobs well, but rather a negative and sadistic one in making others suffer for their human shortcomings (provoking paranoid tendencies, for example, through the sale of spotted horses, and exploiting a dehumanizing pruriency by making a voyeuristic spectacle of an idiot's love for a cow). Those who argue that Emersonian transcendentalism *necessarily* leads to barbarous self-gratification simply reveal their own Snopesian lack of vision. Faulkner manages, without urging the claims of traditional religion, the same contrast in Flem Snopes, Will Varner, and Ratliff that Elgin Groseclose in *Ararat* presents through Hashim Farouk Bey, Amos Lyle, and Paul Markov.

Closely connected with the championing of individualism is a distrust of any kind of government that verges on a contempt for the organized state. This contempt for government may actually be responsible for the ardent praise of individualism, for all three authors distrusted above all else that which threatened to reduce men to automata. They felt the passionate championing of individualism necessary to prevent men from being reduced to robots.

At first, even though *The Hamlet* sheds light on the conduct of government in Mississippi, it does not seem aimed directly at the corrupt state. On the one occasion, however, that the actors in the novel come into direct contact with an agency of the government outside Frenchman's Bend—the trial in which Mrs. Tull and Mrs. Armstid attempt to recover damages (pp. 367–80)—the court is depicted as frustrating rather than administering justice, because its operation is hopelessly bogged down by legal technicalities that aid unscrupulous persons like Flem Snopes, but fail to protect the ignorant and innocent. Even the brief satirical account of the state university's debut in football suggests Faulkner's vision of the government's corruption and incompetence. Although he did not dwell on government to the extent that Hemingway and Steinbeck did, the picture of the agencies of the state throughout *The Hamlet* make it clear that Faulkner did not think that the troubled individual could obtain much assistance from an organization helpless to resist the rise of Snopesism.

Hemingway's boundless contempt for all government, expressed through the attack on "both houses" in the Spanish Civil War, scarcely needs further comment. This novelist agrees perhaps most completely of the three with Lord Acton's famous dictum about the corrupting effect of power. Even the best people, like Pilar, are temporarily corrupted when the most limited power is thrust into their hands. The only difference between the "good guys" and the incorrigible scoundrels is that the virtuous at last become sick of wallowing in their own corruption and seek to escape other men, to fish alone. Their only safety is in woods or water.

Steinbeck's similar position has often been misunderstood because of his sympathetic portrayal of the government-subsidized transient camps in *The Grapes of Wrath*, which is in such marked contrast to Hemingway's depiction of the WPA in *To Have and Have Not*. Steinbeck never suggests, however, that these camps should offer more than temporary relief during emergencies; he never suggests that the government should make work for the people. We must recall, too, the camp manager's comment that the people in the camp had taken his job away from him by assuming responsibilities for self-government. Steinbeck's approval of organized government extended to nothing more complicated than that type represented by the eighteenth-century town meeting in New England. There are constant jibes at bureaucracy throughout *The Grapes of Wrath*. When Grampa Joad dies, the family bitterly reflects that the government is more interested in dead men than living ones (p. 191). The deputy sheriffs, who are the agents of government closest to the people, lead the harassment of the migrants because their superiors either tacitly approve or are indifferent to the migrants' fate. Nowhere in the novel does Steinbeck suggest that government should play a continuing role in shaping people's lives; it should simply protect them so that they can work out their own destinies. Steinbeck—like Tom Paine in *Common Sense*—conceives of the government as nothing more than a police force, and he objects that corrupt police are functioning improperly by working against some people rather than with all people.

All three novelists are profoundly suspicious of any organized government larger than that in which the governors and the governed could be brought face-to-face with each other. Hemingway avoids many of the problems of the conflicts that arise within governments during the prosecution of a war by concentrating on a small guerilla band that thrashes out conflicts by direct deliberation among the disputants. Even when parleys with an adjoining group are necessary, they are carried out face-to-face so that the representatives of the two groups can literally keep an eye on each other. As soon as one's back is turned, his representative or even his associates are likely to betray him, as Pablo does when he steals the dynamite caps. It is difficult to reconcile Hemingway's novel with an approval of any state of society more complicated than that in which each roving band is a law unto itself.

Steinbeck, we have seen, is as lyrically satisfied with the extremely primitive and personal form of government of the migrant camps that are set up each night and disbanded the next morning, as he is with the more durable Weedpatch Camp where the migrants choose the controlling body from their own ranks. Every larger and less intimate governmental organization mentioned in the book is pilloried for its mechanistic lack of humanity. Except that Steinbeck's gypsies hanker to settle down in little white houses, they are not much different from the characters that Hemingway presents sympathetically, and even his Pilar longs to settle down again behind friendly lines.

Faulkner's novel is once again less dogmatic and more ambiguous than the other two. It suggests, for one thing, that it is impossible to trust a man even when you deal with him face-to-face, for time after time the characters in *The Hamlet* defraud those with whom they parley directly. Faulkner was less persuaded than his Midwestern and Far Western countrymen of the infallibility of looking a man directly in the eye (one does learn something in the South). Even Faulkner, however, holds up as not necessarily ideal, but as the best form of government available, that provided by Will Varner from his flour-barrel seat to his

"constituents" in the hamlet. Like Hemingway and Steinbeck, he could conceive of the just state only in terms of
the autonomous village of American colonial days (and
even the flour-barrel seat could be corrupted by Flem
Snopes).

All three novelists felt that big government corroded
men's souls. All could subscribe to the view expressed in
Hemingway's description of Robert Jordan: "This was the
greatest gift that he had . . . that ability not to ignore but
to despise whatever bad ending there could be. This
quality was destroyed by too much responsibility for others
or the necessity of undertaking something ill planned or
badly conceived" (p. 393). "Too much responsibility"
destroys man's ability to despise and eschew evil.

I do not mean to cast any aspersion on the venerable
system of pure democracy. Many Americans besides these
three novelists have believed in it and continue to believe
in it, and I feel certain that at least some part of the
reputation of these three rests upon their endorsement of
the political institution upon which American democracy
is based. The objection to the contemporary insistence on
government by town meeting is simply that which Chester
Eisinger makes against the agrarian concepts in *The
Grapes of Wrath*, "I fear that we cannot use and cannot
achieve agrarianism as a formal way of life. . . . The
machine age, or the atomic age, is fastened upon us and
growing apace. . . . We must seek another road to the
independence and security and dignity that we expect
from democracy." [2]

Discussing Hemingway's primitivism in *For Whom the
Bell Tolls*, Allen Guttmann reaches a similar conclusion.

The failure of the Spanish Republic to arm itself and to
achieve political unity meant the coming of a Spanish
version of Fascism. *And*, had the Loyalists succeeded in
their efforts, the Spanish peasants would have been forced
in the process to accept limitations on their famous individ-

ualism; to adopt the mechanized weapons of modern war; to surrender their archaic relationship with the hard, dry Spanish earth; to become members of a technologically-based mass-society that might or might not have evolved eventually into the Marxist utopia. In either case, the result would have been a curtailment of freedom and an increase in repression.[3]

The system, in short, which the three novelists were driven to praise as a result of the loathing with which they viewed the mess in Mississippi, in the United States, and in the world during the thirties was simply impractical for the times about which they wrote. Its very impracticability is suggested by the novels' focusing upon a remote and dying hamlet, a disintegrating and uprooted family, and a deteriorating band of wanderers visited by a foreigner with a death-wish. It is ironic that the three novels were published just as the most highly mechanized war in history was breaking out—a war that would culminate in the creation of a weapon that could put into the hands of one man the power to destroy all the unperceived millions in the world. As a result of the creation of this new method of destruction, man was forced to accept a political responsibility for millions that he could never see face-to-face whether he considered this responsibility "too much" or not. He was also forced to cope with the problems of automation whether or not he felt equal to the demands of the struggle. One of the most important reasons why the end of the thirties marked the end of an era in literary as well as political history is that the events of World War II simply cut the ground out from under the feet of the most influential and inspiring artists of the preceding period. The solutions that they had passionately championed no longer had any applicability.

Not that the authors necessarily supposed that these solutions could have saved the world even when they wrote. All three novels end on a pessimistic note. Flem Snopes has vanquished all his foes and rides unchallenged into Jefferson, leaving the fields strewn with the defeated. The guerilla band in *For Whom the Bell Tolls* appears to be escaping, but Robert Jordan is left to die and old Anselmo, who represents the goodness in man, is already dead. Even though the Joads at the end of *The Grapes of Wrath* have learned their lesson, there is no guarantee that they will survive physically even though their spirit is unquenchable. While both Hemingway and Steinbeck were still hopeful of rousing public sentiment against the totalitarian forces abroad in the world, the bleak endings of their novels suggest that they thought it was too late even for the appeals that they made for readers' good offices. Faulkner, who was most aware of the complexity of the modern predicament, had the least hope for the future. All three novels tacitly imply that man had reached Armageddon, that the end of an era was indeed the end of the world.

Even if World War II simply precipitated a whole host of new problems, it surprised many by resulting not in the predicted destruction of society, but in the smashing of the Fascist automata by the sheer force of an uneasy alliance and technical ingenuity. It also became apparent that if the world could be preserved at all, it would certainly not be by everyone's going back to farm and village. Much as one might yearn for old-fashioned individualism, one was obliged now to accept "too much responsibility" when it was thrust upon him. Those who since 1945 have insisted upon clamoring for the anarchical individualism still fashionable in the thirties, have increasingly appeared a lunatic fringe.

One outstanding distinction of Faulkner, Hemingway, and Steinbeck is that instead of freezing into a position that increasingly alienated them from their times (like Dos Passos and Dalton Trumbo), they have each experienced a change of heart and have attempted—with varying success—to make a statement about the possibility of man's enduring in an atomic age.

These changes came about slowly. The first postwar work of the three novelists was out of step with the times. Faulkner in *Intruder in the Dust* continued to mock fumbling officialdom with his portrayal of the triumph of justice only through the efforts of an old woman and an adolescent in an unlikely tale that editorially denounces outside interference in regional problems. Steinbeck in *The Wayward Bus* came up with a lumbering allegory seeking to prove that the salvation of modern society (represented by a cross section of caricatures) still depends upon the Christlike individual (Juan Chicoy) who leaves the beaten path and indulges in a form of "therapeutic fornication" that brings joy to the receiver rather than the giver. Hemingway, depicting in the dirgelike *Across the River and into the Trees* (the very title loaded with primitivistic implications) the death of a man with *cojones*, seems simply to be saying that it is all over for the world that the author and his wounded colonel have known.

All three novelists passed, like many of their contemporaries, into marked declines, turning more and more to a preoccupation with empty technique (Faulkner's detective stories and *Requiem for a Nun*), an obsession with contrived allegories (Steinbeck's *The Pearl* and *Burning Bright*, and Faulkner's *A Fable*), and restless attempts to recapture the good life that had vanished (Hemingway by traveling, Steinbeck by returning to Cannery Row in *Sweet Thursday*). The nadir was reached in 1954 in the last-named novel, in which the grotesque "Old Jingleballicks" champions individualism and denounces government in the same manner as Harold Gray's "Little Orphan Annie" comic strip.

Even earlier in the fifties, however, these three novelists whom critics had begun to write off as no longer of continuing significance began to display a remarkably phoenix-like power to recover their ability to speak to the times. After some years of silence, Hemingway brought forth in 1952 his short but enormously popular fable, *The Old Man and the Sea*, in which he suggested at least that the resolute Stoic might survive the destruction of his world and his hopes, admirably enough to provide an inspiring example to the rising generation. Once again Hemingway's characters move in almost as great isolation from the main body of civilization as in *For Whom the Bell Tolls*. But although old Santiago loses the fish he sought and struggled for so long, he is not—like old Anselmo—destroyed by either sharks or a cruel freak of nature. He lives to dream of lions while a boy watches.

Although Faulkner expressed as early as 1950, in his famous speech accepting the Nobel Prize for literature, his belief that man might not only endure, but prevail, he was slow to create a convincing fictional embodiment of the concept. *Requiem for a Nun* and *A Fable* seem attempts at positive statements about man's rejection of evil, but they both show an obsession with the past that gives them the air of anachronistic period pieces. This withdrawal into an irrelevant past is even more marked in *The Town* (1957), the long awaited second volume of the Snopes saga that proved an uneven pastiche of deftly ironic tales written in the thirties, glued together with a soggily told tale of death and dishonor that turns Jefferson into a Peyton Place and suggests a depressing difference in the tale-telling skill of the "old" and "new" Faulkner. Since the final vignette in the novel of the vicious, brute off-spring of the Snopeses offered a vision of a world reduced not just to automatism, but to the foulest kind of animal-ism, the passing years seemed simply to have confirmed the misanthropy that Faulkner (like Quentin Compson in *Absalom, Absalom!*) had struggled to hold out against during his greatest creative years in the thirties.

With *The Mansion* (1959), last volume of the Snopes

trilogy, came evidence at last that the Nobel speech was more than high-sounding words. Faulkner finally found dramatic means to embody the renewed faith that he had expressed in interviews in Japan and Virginia. Seemingly invincible Snopesism was suggested ultimately to be destructible, even though the destruction would have to come from within, not from without. Flem Snopes parries all the thrusts of his opponents, but he is destroyed at last when his own mistake in betraying a kinsman catches up with him at a time when he has become bored with his triumphs. Faulkner, comfortable at last in Charlottesville after years of scorn, brought himself around to the belief that within antihuman forces lie the slow germinating seeds of their own destruction. Remarkably, he still had the creative vigor to give this new vision the dramatic embodiment he had the old. Although he had evidently contemplated a trilogy of books about the Snopeses for many years, there is no suggestion even in *The Town* that when he had begun the history he contemplated turning it at last into a tragi-farcical account of the long deferred triumph of "something that don't want nothing but to walk and feel the sun."

Steinbeck had become optimistic about the possibility of man's enduring, much earlier than the other two novelists, but as late as *The Short Reign of Pippin* IV (1957), he had resolutely refused to allow his characters to come to terms with the modern world. Steinbeck had mellowed to the extent that he had allowed Pippin to flaunt authority and survive, whereas Danny in *Tortilla Flat*, Doc Burton in *In Dubious Battle*, and Jim Casy in *The Grapes of Wrath* had been destroyed for their defiant gestures; but Pippin survives, like Doc in *Cannery Row*, only by turning his back on society and retreating to his scientific hermitage. Steinbeck could not bring himself to depict the sensitive individual as able to survive without withdrawing from the modern world.

The first sign of a change came with a short story, "How Mr. Hogan Robbed a Bank," that appeared in the *Atlantic Monthly* (March, 1956), even before *Pippin* was published. This delightful tale depicts the "little man" as able to put something over on the impersonal financial institutions that had destroyed so many little men in *The Grapes of Wrath*. This story provided the nucleus for *The Winter of Our Discontent* (1961), although in this more pretentious work Steinbeck no longer found it expedient to allow his heroic grocer to carry off a bank robbery. The whole business of the bank robbery seems an irrelevancy, in fact, in the story of Ethan Allen Hawley's struggle to accept the conditions of success in a corrupt world.

Feeling that in order to frustrate the greedy schemes of miscreants who are responsible for his own family's fortune evaporating, he must adopt their tactics and exploit a friend, Hawley is driven to the brink of suicide by his despair at the loss of his own innocence. At the last moment, however, he recognizes that even suicide will be simply a form of self-gratification, because he has an obligation to struggle to survive for the sake of his children, "else another light might go out." [4]

Steinbeck's cheerless conclusion that once more repeats the sentiment of T. S. Eliot's Gerontion that "what is kept must be adulterated," can hardly be described as a complete reconciliation with the world, but it does show that it may be possible, even if painful, for the individual to sustain himself in a corrupt society. Significantly, responsibility for the succeeding generation (that Robert Jordan was reluctant to bring into the world) has been treated in the last or latest work of all three of these authors as the reason for man's reluctantly acknowledging the necessity for his coming to terms with a corrupt world. Despite the fears of many in the thirties, the world did not end because irresponsible people had made a mess of it. One cannot wash his hands of the present without betraying the future. Old Santiago in *The Old Man and the Sea* must provide an example for the boy, Ratliff in *The Mansion* finds "his son in spirit and intellect" in Chick Mallison, Ethan Allen Hawley in *The Winter of Our Discontent* learns that he must take the responsibility for his children.

In their latest novels all three of these American novelists, who won the Nobel Prize largely because of their distinguished work in the thirties, moved away from their earlier position that there was no hope at all for the individual in the complex and ruthless modern state to a somewhat rueful recognition that this state, like the sharks that plague old Santiago, is here to stay and that the individual must develop like Santiago the fortitude, like Mink Snopes the patience, and like Ethan Allen Hawley the ability to endure loss of innocence in order to survive in a situation from which he cannot practically disassociate himself.

Perhaps the principal reason why few younger novelists have risen to challenge the eminence of these giants of the thirties is that too often the writers have spent their energies advocating a form of disassociation from society that their predecessors had at last learned was simply an escapist illusion.

# 7 EPILOGUE:
## BEGINNERS' LUCK

SINCE MOST "promising" first novelists fail to fulfill their promise, they provide no reliable guide to the literary situation during various periods. We at once notice the failure of those who began their careers as the thirties ended, to establish a tradition of social fiction that would replace the waning traditions of the "lost generation" and the "proletarians" of the early thirties,[1] particularly since the most talked about first novel of the years that I am considering has not, like many of its predecessors, lost its power with the passage of time.

Richard Wright was not a newcomer to the literary scene when *Native Son* was published in 1940. He had been contributing to *New Masses* and other periodicals sympathetic to communism since he had become acquainted in the early thirties with the members of the Chicago John Reed Club. He had worked for several years on the WPA Federal Writers' Project, and his collection of short stories, *Uncle Tom's Children*, had won a prize that *Story* magazine had offered for the best book by a member of the government project. This work had also established Wright's reputation as a powerful delineator of the shocking conditions under which Negroes lived in the South. *Native Son* was not even a first novel, although a predecessor, *Lawd Today*, was not published until several years after Wright's death in 1960.

If *Lawd Today* had been published before *Native Son*, it might have lessened expectations, fostered by Wright's short stories, that his most famous work would be essentially a sociological study of conditions in Chicago's Negro ghetto, but it might also have weakened the stunning impact of the more powerful and emotionally gripping work that the public received as a first novel.

*Lawd Today* describes one day, during the thirties, in the disorderly life of Jake Johnson, for nine years a mail sorter in the main Chicago post office. On this particular day several of Jake's long standing difficulties come to a head, but it marks neither the beginning nor the end of his problems. We learn that Jake no longer loves his tumor-ridden wife, that he is in danger of losing his job for drinking on duty, dodging debts, and beating his wife, that the money he earns dribbles through his fingers to purchase policy tickets, political influence, and prostitutes' favors. The story ends as it begins with a violent quarrel between Jake and his wife; between bouts we see him idling with a pal who has venereal disease, borrowing money, lying about his situation, doing his job poorly, and being rolled in a honky-tonk night club of the borrowed money with which he has been giving a party.

The incidents are scarcely remarkable in themselves, and there is no semblance of a plot to hold together these episodes that are reproduced in painstaking detail. The remarkable thing about the work, however, is that not once in the rowdily tragic account does the author intrude with comments. Jake's situation is completely dramatized, so that the work serves as an entirely successful specimen of the technique that Wayne Booth calls *showing*. What is shown as we follow Jake through a maze of lies, evasions, and self-indulgences is his own absolute irresponsibility and his braggadocio in the face of his inability to cope with the net of circumstances closing about him. He is as much as Fitzgerald's Tom Buchanan *the* representative figure of his era, and it is small wonder that publishers of the time could not accept Wright's undeviatingly candid portrayal of the personification of the times. We finish the book wondering what will happen to Jake and knowing that it can't be good. Yet our sympathies have been aroused despite all his inadequacies and vices, because Wright's technique forces us to share his experience.

*Lawd Today* is likely to be misunderstood, for it is only in a very limited sense a "Negro" novel. While a few of Jake's particular troubles are the result of the Negro's confinement in a ghetto, this type of person's fate would not be much different regardless of race, color, or residence. Holding as he does a steady and, for depression times, well paying government job, Jake is better off than many of his contemporaries. His security is not threatened by outsiders, but by his own temperament. *Lawd Today* is an appalling revelation of man destroying himself.

The warning explicit in *Lawd Today*, that was not available to the first readers of *Native Son*, is that one is ill-advised to assume that any of Wright's characters are spokesmen for the author or that his Negro character's problems are necessarily of racial origin. Bigger Thomas in *Native Son* is, like Jake Johnson, a "bad nigger," and both books show how completely Wright could present with utter detachment a story about a character with whom he did not agree. Much misunderstanding of *Native Son* has resulted from Wright's creating the impulsive action and confused thoughts of Bigger Thomas with such extraordinary success that the reader becomes emotionally identified with a character whose behavior he would objectively consider repulsive.

The novel with which early reviewers most frequently compared *Native Son* was Theodore Dreiser's *An American Tragedy*, which also dealt with a poor and irresponsible young man who is executed for his part in a girl's death. The parallel, however, is not really close, despite the superficial similarity of the incidents. Even though Dreiser's Clyde Griffiths was not technically responsible for the death of his pregnant ex-sweetheart, he had carefully plotted to murder her, and had taken her out on a fatal boating trip with the idea of disposing of her. He wanted her out of the way, furthermore, because she had become a liability when he calculated that he might have a chance to marry an heiress. Society was responsible for his criminal intentions because it inspired him with meretricious ideals.

Bigger Thomas' murder of the daughter of a white family that has given him a job is entirely unpremeditated; it is the consequence of spur-of-the-moment hysteria induced by a situation into which Bigger is forced by the arrogantly irresponsible girl and her naïve Communist boy friend. Society's fault is that it punishes Bigger for the uncommitted crime of rape, as a result of its stereotype of the oversexed Negro. Wright's characters (except the young Communist) are not Dreiser's Rousseauesque innocents in a world of corrupt institutions; they are deranged individuals whose difficulties are not discerned, because they are viewed as stereotypes rather than unique individuals. Wright is more sophisticated as both man and artist than Dreiser; the failure of some critics to perceive the difference shows their own staggering lack of sophistication.

The book that truly most nearly parallels Wright's appeared a few years later from a quite remote source. Nick Aaron Ford, in one of the most perceptive accounts of Wright's disappointing later work, demonstrates that after the novelist moved permanently to Paris in 1946, his writing reflected the tenets of the existentialists whom he had come to know quite well. What Ford does not point out is that Wright had displayed existentialist tendencies before going to Paris and that there are striking similarities between *Native Son* and Albert Camus's *The Stranger*.[2]

These similarities are especially related to what Ford calls the second existentialist principle illustrated in Wright's later novel *The Outsider*—that in a godless world, "there is no reality beyond subjectivity. Man can be no more nor less than what he conceives himself to be." [3] One possible consequence of this attitude is that exhibited by Doctor Rieux in Camus's *The Plague*, who believes that the "right road" is "fighting against creation as he found it." [4] Rieux accepts a godless creation as a positive challenge to his ability to preserve other men so that society may continue; Bigger and Meursault, on the other hand, react negatively to the lack of a controlling force and are increasingly destructively detached from society. Meursault indicates the extent of his isolation when he remarks that he had "rather lost the habit of noting [his] feelings" (p. 80) [5] and that he had "never been able really to regret anything in all [his] life" (p. 127). Ultimately his lack of stereotyped sentiments common to men in his society results in his conviction and destruction, not so much for the murder of an Arab (How much did the French in Algeria care about the Arabs?) as for failing to display the filial respect characteristic of his culture during his mother's funeral. His inability to be anything except what he conceives himself to be is shown, too, by his reflection that he "never could get reconciled" to thinking of himself as a criminal (p. 87).

Bigger Thomas's alienation is stressed by Wright in "How 'Bigger' Was Born," his own commentary on the work that remains the most useful guide to it. After explaining that the character developed from his observation during his youth of a number of bullying "Biggers," Wright points out that "through some quirk of circumstance, [each] had become estranged from the religion and folk culture of his race" [6] (just as Meursault has). Abundant evidence of Bigger's condition is also provided in the novel itself, which shows that, like Meursault, the young

Negro has lost the habit of harboring feelings or regrets concerning others.

> He hated his family because he knew that they were suffering and that he was powerless to help them. He knew that the moment he allowed himself to feel to its fulness how they lived, the shame and misery of their lives, he would be swept out of himself with fear and despair. So he held toward them an attitude of iron reserve; he lived with them, but behind a wall, a curtain. And toward himself he was even more exacting. He knew that the moment he allowed what his life meant to enter fully into his consciousness, he would either kill himself or someone else. So he denied himself and acted tough. (p. 9) [7]

Bigger here is not just a mechanism responding naturalistically to environmental forces, but a man neither more nor less than he conceives himself to be. His sense of isolation is increased by the murder, which actually gives him his first sense of an identity that he has achieved for himself.

> He had murdered and had created a new life for himself. It was something that was all his own, and it was the first time in his life he had had anything that others could not take from him. Yes; he could sit here calmly and eat and not be concerned about what his family thought or did. He had a natural wall from behind which he could look at them. (p. 90)

Like Meursault, Bigger belongs to a special breed of people who cannot bear the sensation of society crowding in on them and obliterating their subjective identity. The existentialists were not the first to perceive this type. Almost a century earlier, Melville had a character in *The Confidence Man* describe a particular type of frontiersman.

> "The backwoodsman is a lonely man. He is a thoughtful man. He is a man strong and unsophisticated. Impulsive, he is what some might call unprincipled. . . . With few companions, solitude by necessity his lengthened lot, he

stands the trial—no slight one, since, next to dying, solitude, rightly borne, is perhaps of fortitude the most
rigorous test. But not merely is the backwoodsman content
to be alone, but in no few cases is anxious to be so. The
sight of smoke ten miles off is provocation to one more
remove from man, one step deeper into nature." [8]

Bigger Thomas' similarity to this frontier type becomes
climactically apparent when, in one of his final speeches,
Bigger at last reveals himself to the lawyer who has
attempted to help him.

> "But really I never wanted to hurt nobody. That's the
> truth, Mr. Max. I hurt folks 'cause I felt I had to; that's all.
> They was crowding me too close; they wouldn't give me no
> room. Lots of times I tried to forget 'em, but I couldn't.
> They wouldn't let me." (p. 355)

More than one modern writer has decried the frustration of the individual resulting from the closing of the
frontier and other events depriving man of solitude.
Wright's point about Bigger as not just Negro, but human
being, is that the plight of the antisocial individual is
doubly frustrating when society crowds him—as it does the
Negro—into ghettos that constrict his opportunities and
movements even more than those of others. Meursault
manages to survive longer than Bigger because he is a
member of a more privileged class, safe until another
person begins pressing the claims of a friendship that
Meursault has not sought. Bigger, however, has no chance
at all, for according to the dominant society's stereotype
Negroes are gregarious and could not be antisocial.

Despite Wright's vaster canvas and weakness for steno-
graphic transcripts of conversations and Camus's more
compressed and elliptical style making the novels quite
different in bulk, the slender basic plots are significantly
similar. Both men's isolation from the norms of their
society is shown at the beginning of the novel through
their attitudes toward their families, especially their moth-

ers. Both men are forced by someone else into a situation that leads to their committing murder (Bigger by the headstrong girl, Meursault by the suspected pimp), each is forced into friendship with a person that the aggressor is too self-preoccupied to recognize as perhaps dangerously antisocial. Both men commit murder without premeditation while under enormous mental strain (Meursault from the overbearing heat of the sun; Bigger, curiously, from the compromising darkness). Both, thereafter, instead of taking refuge in flight, commit frightful acts of irrational violence (Meursault empties the revolver into the prostrate Arab's body; Bigger chops off Mary's head in order to stuff her body into a furnace). Neither can really conceive of the fate in store for him. Bigger cannot believe that he will really be suspected; Meursault has "always a vague hope that something would turn up, some agreeable surprise" (p. 89). At both trials much weight is placed on what should be an inadmissible irrelevancy—Meursault's behavior at his mother's funeral and Bigger's supposititious rape of the white girl he killed. Both are hated not so much for their crimes as for their indifference to the conventions of the community. Bigger is actually granted, on several occasions, what Meursault finally comes to hope for after he recognizes "the benign indifference of the universe"— "a huge crowd of spectators and that they should greet me with howls of execration" (p. 154).

In outline the two novels part company only at the end, when Bigger at last reaches from behind his wall to try to establish emotional communication with another man while Meursault longs for the howling crowd whose fury Bigger has already experienced. Even this last difference may not signal so much, however, the authors' differing concepts of the outcome of the existential dilemma of the "self-made man" whom the community destroys rather than honors, as simply Wright's recognition of Bigger's incapacity to arrive at any understanding of so vast an abstraction as "the benign indifference of the universe" that comforts Meursault. The two stories certainly project basically identical visions of the antisocial man's plight in an oppressive society, and it is especially noteworthy that both novels deal with members of minority groups, even though Camus does not stress that his character belongs to a politically dominant rather than a subjugated minority.

Stressing the similarity of Wright's detailed and explicit text to Camus's evocative and often cryptic fable, admittedly oversimplifies the story of Bigger Thomas by ignoring its racial and political overtones. These have, however, already been extensively discussed in criticisms of the work, while what can be called the existential framework of the tale has not been sufficiently exposed. The comparison between the authors makes us realize, too, that Wright in *Native Son* was not so much interested in protesting against specific social conditions as in pointing out that the kind of flight from urban society that we have seen many novelists advocating during the thirties was not even available to the Negro minority. Wright's recognition that men might be caught in a social situation where they must either compromise or be destroyed shows, too, that he had a vision that uniquely equipped him to deal with the problems of the post-World War II world that so long stymied some of the major novelists of the thirties.

Why then did he fail to develop as a novelist after making such an auspicious start? He mentioned in 1940 that he was working on a novel about woman's position in American society, but he published no more novels for fifteen years after his initial success. His later fiction never found the same favor as his earlier, either, and I suspect that it is less effective for one of the reasons that Steinbeck's is after 1945 — Wright lost immediate touch with the sights and sounds of the world of the American Negro that he reproduced with such extraordinary fidelity in his early works. Even though *Lawd Today* and *Native Son* had universal implications, their impact was the result of Wright's translation of a universal dilemma into the terms of a time and place that he knew intimately.

He was also apparently a victim of his own articulateness. After the enormous success of *Native Son*, tempting distractions prevented his devoting himself to fiction. He helped Paul Green dramatize *Native Son* for staging by Orson Welles, and he later played Bigger himself in a motion picture version produced in Argentina. He wrote newspaper and magazine articles about the American Negro and contributed introductions to others' books. He became, in short, an intellectual spokesman for his race. Then he turned to writing about his own early years in *Black Boy*. Such efforts could not but interfere with his career, for as he himself explained, "the conditions of creative writing are essentially lonely, subjective, individualistic, intense, and concentrated." [9] Ironically, his novel had made him too celebrated to continue writing fiction.

## *ii*

Quite a different kind of distraction accounted for the failure of a young Italian-American, who wrote one of the most effective social novels at the end of the thirties, to fulfill his promise.

Probably Frank Norris is just one of many who has told the pathetic tale of a naïve youngster whose first novel about the crude but goodhearted people of the primitive world of his childhood is an unexpected success. Lionized in New York, the hero of Norris' "Dying Fires" is advised to forsake his rude origins and live among the literary Bohemians writing about genteel folk. When he succumbs, his works fail and his new friends abandon him to pursue a newer *wunderkind*. Back home he finds that he cannot recapture his inspiration.

Although this tearjerker sounds more like a hack writer's daydream than actual history, almost exactly what happens in Norris' fable did happen to Pietro di Donato, whose first novel, *Christ in Concrete*, deservedly received in 1939 a reception overshadowed only by that accorded *Native Son* a few months later.

Like Wright, di Donato came from a minority culture—the large Italian immigrant colony in Hoboken, New Jersey. It took little imagination to turn his early life into a novel. When he was twelve, his father, a bricklayer who was about to make the down payment on a house that would get his family out of a tenement, was buried alive during the collapse of a building on which he was working. Pietro had to give up school in order to support his mother and eight younger children. He became a bricklayer like his father, but continued to study engineering in night school and to read Zola and Dostoevsky. After fulfilling his father's ambition to move the family to its own house on Long Island, he also created from the events leading to his father's death, a short, poetic tale, "Christ in Concrete," which appeared in *Esquire* and was selected by Edward O'Brien as the best short story of 1937.

This initial success encouraged di Donato to take a year off to extend the original story into a novel based on his efforts to provide the income that would help his mother hold the family together. This moving chronicle of births, marriages, accidents, and deaths in the swarming slums became a selection of the Book-of-the-Month Club, and the author found himself suddenly transformed from a construction worker at the New York World's Fair into a celebrity in demand as a lecturer in Manhattan's vanity fair.

For once the blurb writers spoke truly. *Christ in Concrete* is one of those rare things—a beautiful book. We know little about the formation of di Donato's style and what, if any, assistance he received from editors; but somehow he succeeded in transmuting the nervously energetic language of a sensitive man suspended between two cultures into a literary prose unduplicated in American letters. A large measure of his distinction results from his difference from the usual social novelist. Most men who write about underprivileged minorities belong to the handful of dynamic protestants who will not uncomplainingly accept the underdog role that society forces upon them. They are like Bigger Thomas, but their energies have been constructively channeled into art or at least propaganda rather than destructively vented—like Bigger's—in violence and murder.

By far the larger number of members of these minorities, however, unless goaded beyond endurance by tyrants from outside their ranks or by spellbinders within, endure their distasteful lot quietly and fearfully. Usually this majority is inarticulate. Di Donato speaks, however, for these silent people and offers an unusual vision not of the self-motivated rebel scaling slum walls, but of the more common timorous, superstitious, acquiescent tenement dwellers, suffering, without hope of redress, at the hands of unscrupulous employers and indifferent governmental timeservers, remaining loyal to a traditional church while seeking from spiritualists the comfort it denies, and grasping at such simple and fleeting pleasures as occasional good fortune affords them.

*Christ in Concrete* is a tale of the poor, the confused, the wretched, written not from outside, but from within—not by one seeking out of hatred to whip up revolutionary fervor, but motivated rather by an overwhelming love for his clan, his culture, and his calling. Critics who complain of the lack of serious modern love stories have overlooked *Christ in Concrete*. Although it touches only lightly and delicately on a youth's first sexual stirrings, it is a rare expression of love as a modern way of life.

Yet it is unmistakably an important social novel. Di Donato is too sensitive and perceptive an observer to be unaware of the shortcomings of his society. His novel ends as it begins with a sickening death that results from a greedy contractor's desire to cut corners. Over every episode hangs the shadow of the forces that seek to oppress and destroy the boisterous, lively spirit of the unsophisticated immigrants who must provide for their constantly expanding families. Di Donato constantly intimates the social significance of his novel by his personification of the Job, which is actually the dominant character in the book because of the way in which the welfare and very lives of simple people depend upon the vagaries and caprices of dangerous and ill-paid employment.

Because the story of the hordes of immigrants responsible for the growth of the late-nineteenth-century and early-twentieth-century American slums is an important chapter in our national history that has too rarely provided a basis for artistically successful fiction by an insider, *Christ in Concrete* has enduring value as an almost unique artistic document and as a social novel that succeeds far better than many violent protest stories because of the way in which the muted protests make the careful reader discover for himself the underlying plight of those who bravely tried to cling to a tradition.

Because of di Donato's extraordinary achievement in developing a brisk, mature literary style without losing the unsophisticated viewpoint of his working-class culture, he promised to make a distinctive contribution to American literature. Unfortunately his background provided him with no protection against a sudden access of fortune and the flattering attentions of a literary clique intent upon lionizing a "primitive." We can conceive of the blandishments showered upon the naïve young construction worker from Dorothy Canfield Fisher's Book-of-the-Month club promotional brochure, which begins "When will we ever have the good fortune to see again such a white blackbird as this book about wage-earners by one of them" and advises, among other things, that "not Breughel himself ever gave us a more hilarious rejoicing at a wedding-feast." [10]

Years after his disappearance from the New York literary scene, di Donato recalled that his book had earned a hundred thousand dollars, but that he had squandered the money on "material madness"—restaurants, women, clothes, cars.[11] When the money was gone, the new friends disappeared, and he was too nervously exhausted to resume writing. After wandering about the country for a number of years, he finally married and returned to his old construction trade on Long Island. Many years later he attempted to resume his literary career. A flurry of activity in the early fifties resulted in a few more stories drawn from childhood experiences; but it was not until late in the fifties, almost twenty years after his first success, that he began to publish extensively—new novels, articles about Italian-Americans, a highly emotional biography of Mother Cabrini, the first American saint. None of these works, however, has attracted anything like the attention that *Christ in Concrete* did. The writings of a disillusioned and disheartened middle-aged man inevitably lack the poetic exuberance of a youth whose outstanding asset was his lack of inhibition in reconstructing the private emotions of a generally shy and secretive people.

### iii

After considering the failure of Wright and di Donato to live up to the brilliant starts they had made, I am relieved to be able to wind up this highly selective survey on an upbeat. The same month that saw the publication of *The Grapes of Wrath* witnessed also the release of the first novel of a man whose reputation was to rest principally upon the widely discussed fiction that he would write after World War II.

Robert Penn Warren was, even in 1939, no newcomer to

the American reading audience. Back in 1929, when only 24, he had won respect for his scrupulously documented account of abolitionist leader John Brown, and during the thirties he had gained enormous prestige as a poet and as an editor of the distinguished *Southern Review* at Louisiana State University. With his coeditor Cleanth Brooks, he had become best known of all, however, for the unusually influential textbook, *Understanding Poetry* (1938), which is generally recognized and widely honored for having revolutionized the teaching of literature in American colleges by replacing a timeworn combination of gush and gossip with the kind of close readings identified with the New Criticism. Because of his stature as critic, poet, scholar, and editor, Warren's *Night Rider* was scrutinized with unusual interest by those who generally regard the torrent of new fiction with disdain.

As Harry Warfel points out, the novel deals basically with problems that "are moral rather than social"; [12] yet it fits the definition of social novel that I am employing as well as any work that I have considered because it deals with a specific and tragic series of events in the region where Warren was born, in a way that illuminates the history that one can piece together from other sources. Although *Night Rider* deals with events that occurred, like those in Faulkner's *The Hamlet*, near the turn of the century, it is distinctly not a "historical" novel. It does not attempt to restage the actual sequence of events during the "Black-Patch War" in the tobacco-growing region between Paducah, Kentucky, and Clarksville, Tennessee, so much as to make the reader uncomfortably aware of the parallel between the events that destroyed the society of this remote and isolated region and those that threatened, when Warren wrote, to destroy the whole Western world.

Some of the early reviewers complained that the novel did not present enough historical background information; but Warren, like Faulkner, was not fictionalizing history.

He touched upon actual events only enough to show how they affected the individuals whose motivations and actions most concerned him. From other scattered accounts of a shameful period that Kentucky historians have not chosen to dwell upon, we can see that Warren particularly used his license as novelist to compress many different events happening over a period of years into a compact, uncluttered narrative. The raid of the night riders on Bardsville just before New Year's combines incidents that occurred in three of the largest actual raids on Trenton (December, 1905), Princeton (November 30, 1906), and Hopkinsville, Kentucky (1907). Warren borrows details from history, but reshapes them.[13] The pursuit of parallels is unimportant. What matters to Warren is that agents representing European tobacco monopolies colluded to keep prices of Kentucky black tobacco disastrously low. To protect themselves, the tobacco growers organized, as they do in *Night Rider*, first a cooperative marketing association, and then a "protective" association of masked raiders to force proud and stubbornly independent small farmers, who didn't want any man telling them what to do, to join the organization or else have their crops destroyed, their barns burned, and themselves beaten or killed.

To Warren, the most important consideration is the influence of these events upon an able, ambitious, but aimless young lawyer, trained in Philadelphia, who out of homesickness drifts back to his native region to marry, farm a bit on the old homestead, and set up practice. His talents are quickly recognized by an apoplectic paranoid ironically named Christian, who names his dogs after ladies he has known, treats his charming daughter like a dog, and rants like Melville's Captain Ahab for vengeance upon the monsters who have dared offer him an offensively low price for his tobacco. Because the lawyer cannot think of any good reason to resist, and because he is vaguely motivated by a force that he cannot name (but which anyone in the days of Vance Packard can recognize as the drive for power and prestige), he joins first the directing board of the marketing association and then the night-riding "protective" association. His career of intimidating his neighbors and blowing up warehouses is capped when he is responsible for the killing of one of the more viciously belligerent of his poor neighbors, the very man the lawyer had earlier gotten acquitted from a possibly justified charge of murder.

Warren traces with painstaking skill the course of lawyer Perse Munn's brutalization. It leads first to his separation from his inoffensive, devoted wife after he attacks her sexually the night of the killing, then to the loss of his ancestral homestead to a rival band of thugs who want to clear the neighborhood of Negroes, and at last to the responsibility for the deaths of a hero-worshipping son of an old friend—after the boy follows Munn into the night riders—and his cohort Christian, who is fatally stricken when he discovers that Munn has been sleeping with Christian's daughter during the nights that he has hospitably been invited to stay with them. At last, with one of those colossal double ironies that have become the trademark and at times the failure of Warren's art, Munn is shot to death while being pursued for the killing of a man he did not kill, just a few minutes after he has found himself unable to kill a treacherous ex-Senator, whose betrayal of the tobacco marketing cooperative inspired the organization of the night riders.

Although Warren never offends the reader by underlining the obvious moral of this bloody tale, the parallels between events in Kentucky's Pennyrile early in the century and those in Europe between the World Wars is inescapable. What had started out with much smug self-congratulation as movements to right wrongs that groups out of power had suffered in Germany, Italy, and Spain turned—as the leaders of the oppressed gained power—into vendettas aimed at increasing, extending, and perpetuating the power of these very leaders. When their success inspires rival partisans to organize and emulate the successful tactics, the whole region, as later the world, becomes infested with bands of destroyers that reduce the place that had winked at a little lawlessness in a good cause into a chaos.

Many novelists, however, have depicted the horrors of unleashed terrorism—its destructive effects upon the community and its corrosive effects upon those who realize too late where movements in which they have been thoughtlessly caught up are headed. Warnings abounded especially at the end of the thirties. Why was Robert Penn Warren, almost alone among the socially conscious novelists, able to emerge after World War II a more widely acclaimed writer than he had been in 1939, while most others coasted on their reputations or slipped out of sight?

I suggest that the answer is that Warren displayed an unusual ability to learn from experience. Two important differences between *Night Rider* and *All the King's Men* (1945), the novel based on Huey Long's reign in Louisiana, show this capacity for change.

The first difference is in the modes of narration. Even early reviewers who spoke reverently of the polish of Warren's style found *Night Rider*—especially the opening chapters—slow moving. Warren failed to meet the one requirement that Henry James had said might be imposed upon the novelist—that of interesting the reader.

Quite possibly this refusal to engage the reader was deliberate. Warren may have felt, like others associated with the Vanderbilt literary group in the twenties, that a writer should not think about readers and that an effort to excite readers' interest would make the novelist guilty of the same vice of lusting for attention and power that he castigated in his story. Whatever his reasons, Warren, still thinking primarily as a poet rather than a novelist, attempted to model his story upon the ancient epics. Homeric influences are apparent, for example, as the narrative is suspended for the insertion of long digressions, often relating the life story of subordinate characters. Even the account of the final pursuit of Perse Munn is held up for twenty pages while Willie Proudfit relates in his own sometimes impenetrable dialect the tale of his rambles in the West. While his story provides an important contrapuntal commentary on Munn's tragic history, Warren makes no concessions in its telling that might render it more palatable to the reader engrossed in his protagonist's downfall.

Following Greek precedent, too, much of the violence occurs offstage: buildings blow up at a distance, and we hear courier reports of beatings and killings. Characters often serve as their own choruses, sharing more of their reflections than their experiences with us. Warren appears to have determined to establish the universal qualities of his provincial Kentuckians by moving them like figures in classic epic or tragedy, and such an intention could have been justified by the perception that the characters in the classics were generally—like his people—crude and barbarous provincials capable of destroying the whole world in an effort to preserve and aggrandize their petty states. If the poetry of the Greek epic and drama was suited to the recital of past violence, why should it not serve for the presentation of violence in our time?

Conventions change. The Greek epics abound in what must have been stereotypes to their auditors; the dramas are ritualistic. The successful bards of ancient Greece must have written in a manner that seemed to their auditors appropriate to fictions. Warren, however, was not writing for the ancient Greeks, and the style of *Night Rider* seems pompous and inflated to the reader accustomed to the staccato style of Hemingway and the lucid simplicity of Steinbeck's prose. There is a striking difference between manner and matter in Warren's first novel. When he came, however, to write *All the King's Men*, he allowed his character Jack Burden to tell the story of his involvement with the dictatorial Willie Stark in his own language, genteel but still contemporary. By so doing, Jack involves the reader in his story as Perse Munn—his bloody tale unfolded by a bloodless voice—cannot in *Night Rider*.

There is an even more important difference in the viewpoint underlying the two novels. In an era whose writers were characterized often by the kind of cynicism and despair that produced *The Hamlet* and *Johnny Got His Gun*, Warren wrote the bitterest novel of all. The extent of the feeling of a nearly inhuman coldness that transcends pessimism is shown by two important related passages, one near the beginning, the other near the end of the novel. Called upon as he starts his career with the tobacco growers' association to address a membership meeting, Munn says, after upsetting the others on the platform with the misleading opening comment, "There is no hope in the Association for you":

> "There is nothing here . . . except what you have brought with you from your homes, wherever they are. There is no hope except the hope you bring here. There is nothing here but an idea. And that idea is dead unless you have brought it life by your long trip here. It does not exist unless you give it life by your own hope and loyalty. . . . That idea will not give you quick comfort. Before it gives you comfort it will give you suffering and privation. And it will not give you anything in payment for your suffering, now or later, unless you give your full loyalty to it. The loyalty you have brought with you here today is everything, it is your only hope." (p. 26) [14]

This speech about the necessity of individuals' banding together and struggling to aid the group that defends their interests might have come, late in *The Grapes of Wrath*, from either Casy or Tom Joad. Perse Munn, however, changes his tune before his death. When he goes to kill the ex-Senator, he tells the intended victim that despite a new mailbox, "You were always nothing. Nothing. Nothing."

The other simply echoes, "Nothing. . . . A man never knows what he is, Perse. You don't know what you are, Perse." Munn is ready with his reply, "I do know. I'm nothing" (p. 456). From his experiences Munn has learned that not only ideas, but men, too, are nothing in themselves. At the end of the book, as he dies, "he drowsily heard the voices down the slope calling emptily, like the voices of boys at a game in the dark" (p. 460). That's life: a game played by those who cannot really perceive each other. Although Munn does not quote Macbeth, his tale is clearly "told by an idiot, full of sound and fury, signifying nothing."

Munn's voice, however, is not the only one heard in *Night Rider*. The faint hope that Warren holds out for man is embedded in the garrulous Willie Proudfit's rambling narrative. Willie has roamed the frontier and observed the shocking violence of the destruction of the buffalo, which he describes with greater poignancy than Warren allows anyone to describe the destruction of men (the buffalo, after all, were not guilty of aspiring). One day, however, while Willie is desperately sick among the Rocky Mountain Indians he has a dream or vision.

"I might been gone, when hit come to me, what I seen. I seen a long road come-en down a hill, and green ever whar. Green grass layen fresh, and trees, maple and elm and sich. And my feet was in the road, and me a-move-en down hit. They was a fire in me, and thirsten. . . . I come down the hill, and seen houses setten off down the valley, and roofs, and the green trees standen. I taken a bend in the road, and thar was a little church, a white church with a bell hangen, and the grass green a-fore hit. Thar was a spring thar, by the church, and I seen hit and run to hit . . . I put my face down to the water, and hit was cool on me. The coolness was in me, and I taken my fill.

"No tellen how long, and I lifted up my head. Thar a girl was sitten." (p. 424)

After he leaves the Indians and returns to Kentucky, he

finds that the place in the vision "Lak hit is, and lak hit come to me that time" is in his native hills (p. 426). The girl is there, too, and he marries her. Thus Warren implies that the only hope for man's recovery is, as Faulkner also suggests in "The Bear," in the renunciation of the temptations of civilization and the acceptance of the simple, unaspiring life in one's native woods.

Yet there is a serpent even in this rural Kentucky Eden, where Perse Munn knows his last days of peace in Willie's company. Proudfit has a nephew Sylvestus.

> He was pious, withdrawing from the others to read a chapter in his Bible every night before going to bed; but in his piety there was a certain nervous and demanding and vindictive quality, as though he would wring from it a final meaning and satisfaction, once and for all. He worked hard in the field with his uncle, with that same nervousness and vindictiveness, not as though he occupied himself with tasks that were a part of the tissue of his being, but as though he wrestled to trip and strike an enemy. . . . Willie Proudfit would say to him, "I seen men like you, Sylvestus, and maybe they be goen on lak you for twenty years. And all of a sudden, they seen the world wasn't no diff'rent, and they'd come nigh a-curse-en hit and theirselves. And from that-air day on, they wouldn't sweat nuthen but bitter sweat. And eat their vittles in bitterness. Or they'd lay down and die." (pp. 386–87)

But Sylvestus does not heed his uncle, so that the old story must repeat itself. Indeed it is Sylvestus who at last drives Munn from the Proudfit farm and who, Munn probably correctly suspects, squeals on him to the troops who pursue and kill him. Unless one is truly born again, as Willie Proudfit is, to return again to one's own native soil and lead a completely unpretentious life, one is indeed depraved in a more total sense than Calvin had in mind when he stressed the term. The philosophy that all attempts at social reform are self-destructive has seldom been more unqualifiedly dramatized.

In *All the King's Men* Warren was to move away from

this stark philosophy as he had moved away from the austere style of *Night Rider*. Jack Burden, after the violent demise of dictator Willie Stark, renounces the home that he has learned is corrupted, but he still observes at least parenthetically that Willie's former Attorney General will get back into politics and that when he does, "I'll be along to hold his coat. I've had some valuable experience in that line." [15]

Warren himself had had some valuable experience along the line of writing novels, and he had learned from them as he implied Jack Burden had from his own writing. Warren had come to recognize that man is a dynamic creature and that no matter how attractive the passive Proudfit philosophy may be, it just isn't practical. Since it took the established novelists of the thirties longer to formulate their new ideas and embody them in satisfactory fictional form than it did Robert Penn Warren, the story of the social novel in postwar America begins with his *All the King's Men* as that of the prewar era ends with his elegiac portrayal of irresponsible ambition in *Night Rider*.

NOTES

1 – The End of an Era

1. *The Last Time I Saw Paris* (New York, 1942), p. 414.

2. The only Utopian novel published in this country in 1939 or 1940 to receive serious critical attention is Granville Hicks and Richard M. Bennett's *The First to Awaken* (New York, 1940). It is adequately discussed in Vernon L. Parrington, Jr., *American Dreams: A Study of American Utopias* (Providence, R.I.; 1947), pp. 211–14.

3. Blake sums up the objection to the "historical" novel and its difference from the novel that I am discussing: "Even at its best . . . the historical novel is a secondary account of the past. . . . The real historian is always impatient with learning history at second hand. He prefers to find out about the past from what he calls primary sources—that is, from the evidence left by the actual witnesses and participants of past events. It is from this point of view that literature and the arts open up the most exciting avenues for exploration." "How to Learn History from Sinclair Lewis and Other Uncommon Sources," *American Character and Culture: Some Twentieth Century Perspectives,* ed. John A. Hague (Deland, Florida; 1964), p. 34.

4. (New York, 1948), p. 754.

5. *Hemingway: The Writer as Artist* (Princeton, 1952), p. xvii.

6. Since Peter Lisca broke the news in "The Hamlet: Genesis and Revisions," *Faulkner Studies* III (Spring, 1954), 5–13, that the novel does have a "grand design," it has become a favorite with myth-minded critics. Thin-skinned critics have shied away, however, from the recognition that the grotesque tale is intensely realistic.

7. "Composition and the Elementary Teacher," *College*

*English*, XXVI (November, 1964), 121. Parkinson points out that the hero's stupidity—like Glenn Spotswood's in *The Adventures of a Young Man*—causes his downfall.

## 2 – A Troubled Section –
## "A Little Sweetening for the Chaps"

1. *Faulkner at Nagano* (Tokyo, 1956), p. 197.
2. *Ibid.*, pp. 13–14.
3. *William Faulkner: The Yoknapatawpha Country* (New Haven, 1963), p. 167.
4. *The Hamlet* (New York, 1940). All page references to this original edition will be incorporated into the text.
5. *Revolt of the Rednecks* (Lexington, Kentucky; 1951), p. 4. All subsequent page references to this invaluable book will be incorporated into the text. I have drawn extensively upon this uniquely detailed, objective account of turn-of-the-century Mississippi politics.
6. Far from feeling remorse about this shameful episode, at least one resident of Kemper County published a long vindication of the lynching, culminating in this argument: "However horrifying were the details of the deaths of Chisholm and Gilmer, and however terrible the circumstances, it must be confessed that all regrets were much pacified by the consideration of the great change in the state of affairs of the county. . . . The county warrants, which, under the Chisholm rule, were as low as thirty cents on the dollar, now rapidly advanced to a high par value, and every kind of business received a new impetus and new encouragement throughout the county." James D. Lynch, *Kemper County Vindicated and a Peep at Radical Rule in Mississippi* (New York, 1879), p. 319.
7. *Lanterns on the Levee* (New York, 1946), pp. 143–44. Percy thought less well of Bilbo. He described "the man responsible for tearing Father's reputation to tatters" as "a pert little monster, glib and shameless, with that sort of cunning common to criminals which passes for intelligence" (p. 148).
8. *Ibid.*, p. 149.
9. A. Wigfall Green, *The Man Bilbo* (Baton Rouge, 1963), pp. 40–41, from a report of the speech in the *Jackson Daily News*, July 7, 1911.
10. John Faulkner, *My Brother Bill* (New York, 1963), p. 270.

11. *Ibid.*, pp. 271–73.

12. (Madison, Wisconsin; 1961), p. 89.

13. Green, *op. cit.*, p. 76.

14. *Ibid.*, p. 90.    15. *Ibid.*

16. *Faulkner at the University*, eds. Frederick L. Gwynn and Joseph L. Blotner (Charlottesville, Virginia; 1959), pp. 108–9.

## 3 — A Troubled Nation —
## "How Nice It's Gonna Be, Maybe, in California"

1. *John Steinbeck* (New York, 1961), p. 107.

2. (New York, *ca.* 1936), p. 149.

3. (New York, 1939). All page references incorporated into the text are to this original edition. The Modern Library and Compass Books editions retain the same pagination.

4. Herbert Agar, "Introduction," *Who Owns America?* (Boston, 1936), p. viii.

5. *John Steinbeck: An Introduction and Interpretation* (New York, 1963), p. 96.

6. *The University of Kansas City Review*, XIV (Winter, 1947), 149.

7. *Ibid.*, p. 150.    8. *Ibid.*, p. 152.    9. *Ibid.*, p. 149.

10. "In Praise of Husbandry," *Agricultural History*, XI (April, 1937), 80.

11. *Ibid.*, p. 93.

12. Henry Higgs, *The Physiocrats* (London, 1897; reprinted Hamden, Connecticut, 1963), p. 21.

13. *The Works of Thomas Jefferson*, ed. Paul Leicester Ford (Federal Edition; New York, 1905), IV, 85–86. Only the name of the edition will be used in subsequent references to it.

14. Federal Edition, IV, 449–50.

15. *The Papers of Thomas Jefferson*, ed. Julian P. Boyd (Princeton, 1950– ), XII, 28, 38. This edition will be the authoritative source for quotations from Jefferson's papers when it is eventually completed. It does not contain the text of the *Notes on Virginia*.

16. Federal Edition, VIII, 372.

17. *Ibid.*, XII, 49.    18. *Ibid.*, XII, 453.

19. *The Papal Encyclicals in Their Historical Context*, ed. Anne Fremantle (New York, 1956), p. 86.

20. *Ibid.*, pp. 187–88.

21. The text of the newspaper stories is reprinted in *A Companion to "The Grapes of Wrath,"* ed. Warren French (New York, 1963). See pp. 85–87.

22. *The Papal Encyclicals in Their Historical Context,* pp. 192, 175.

23. *Gilbert Keith Chesterton* (London, 1945), p. 442.

24. *The Outline of Sanity* (New York, 1927), p. 125.

25. *Ibid.,* p. 133.      26. *Ibid.,* p. 129.

27. *Ibid.,* pp. 235–36.

28. *Faulkner at Nagano* (Tokyo, 1956), p. 77.

29. Dumas Malone (ed.), *Correspondence between Thomas Jefferson and Pierre Samuel du Pont de Nemours, 1798–1817* (Boston, 1930), p. 184.

30. Bradley Gilman, *Back to the Soil* (Boston, 1901), pp. 202–3.

31. Herbert J. Wisbey, Jr., *Soldiers without Swords* (New York, 1955), p. 129.

32. *Ibid.,* p. 133.

33. Henry S. Anderson, "The Little Landers' Land Colonies: A Unique Agricultural Experiment in California," *Agricultural History,* V (October, 1931), 140.

34. *Ibid.,* p. 142.      35. *Ibid.,* pp. 149–50.

36. *Ibid.,* pp. 143–44.

37. *Arena,* XXXVIII (August, 1907), 212.

38. *Dial,* XLIII (August 1, 1907), 67.

39. *The Distribution Age* (New York, 1927), p. iv.

40. *Ibid.,* p. 198.

41. *This Ugly Civilization* (New York, 1929), p. 3.

42. *Ibid.,* p. 15.      43. *Ibid.,* pp. 135–36.

44. *Ibid.,* p. 359.

45. "One Way Out," *New Republic,* LIX (July 17, 1929), 223–25; (July 24, 1929), 252–56; (July 31, 1929), 281–83.

46. *Flight from the City* (New York, 1933), pp. 94–95.

47. "Homesteads, Inc.," *New Republic,* LXXVII (November 29, 1933), 77.

48. *Flight from the City,* p. 147.

49. *Ibid.,* pp. 161, 158.      50. *Ibid.,* p. 142.

51. John Chamberlain, "Blueprints for a New Society," *New Republic,* CII (January 1, 1940), 13–16.

52. Ross J. S. Hoffman, "The Totalitarian Régimes: An Essay in Essential Distinctions," *American Review,* IX (September, 1937), 338.

53. "Land Tenure," *American Review*, VII (October, 1936), 561, 563.

54. "The Next Depression," *American Review*, IX (Summer, 1937), 214.

55. *New York Times*, November 2, 1938, p. 5.

56. *Ibid.*, May 5, 1940, pp. 1, 45.

57. *Ibid.*, September 16, 1943, 5.

58. "Getting Down to Earth: A College Graduate's Plans for the Future," *Forum*, LXXXVIII (July, 1932), 60–61.

59. "Letters from an Amateur Farmer to His Brother," *Saturday Evening Post*, CCV (October 8, 1932), 27–28.

60. *Five Acres* (New York, 1935), pp. 5–6.

61. "The Small Farm Secures the State," *Who Owns America?*, pp. 244–45.

62. *R. F. D.* (New York, 1938), p. 100. The description of the decor of the outhouse is omitted from the condensation of the book in the *Reader's Digest*, XXXIII (August, 1938), 113–27. *R. F. D.* was also selected for inclusion as title D–107 in the Armed Services Edition, produced by the Council on Books in Wartime for free distribution among servicemen. On the back cover of this edition it is observed that "Everyone who has nourished a secret dream of getting back to the land will read this book with eager interest, and will find realistic encouragement."

63. *R. F. D.*, p. 51. The most powerful tribute in the *Reader's Digest* condensation is not quoted directly from the book, but is pieced together from isolated statements. The *Digest* version concludes: "Farming is so hazardous and absorbing, so rich in values, that for all those who love the earth and animals and growing things, it offers a deep-rooted and superbly satisfying way of life. . . . many farmers are what in truth all might be—the happiest men on earth." Smart actually uses this last phrase only in explaining, "I may actually be enjoying farming more than most farmers. . . . For instance, I like to look at landscapes, thinking of paintings I have seen or may see. . . . It would also help our farmers to become what—if they only had a little more regimentation and the sweet craziness in the head—they might be, namely, the happiest men on earth" (*R. F. D.*, p. 53).

64. *R. F. D.*, p. 55.

65. (New York, 1938), pp. 188–89.

66. *Weekly Book Review*, April 16, 1944, p. 8.

67. (Norman, Oklahoma; 1942), pp. 261–62.

68. (New York, 1942), p. 199.

69. All page references are to the original edition of *The Egg and I* (New York, 1945).

70. *Seven Lean Years* (Chapel Hill, N. C.; 1939), p. 24.

71. "The Back to the Land Movement," *Rural America*, X (October, 1932), 5.

72. *Seven Lean Years*, p. 107.

73. *Ibid.*, p. 43.

74. (Princeton, 1957), p. 133.

75. *Tomorrow A New World* (Ithaca, N. Y.; *ca.* 1959), p. 327.

76. *Ibid.*, p. 329.

77. *A Place on Earth* (Washington, D. C.; 1942), p. 189.

78. *Ibid.*, p. 190.

79. "Turnips and Romanticism," *Agricultural History*, XII (July, 1938), 249.

80. *University of Kansas City Review*, XIV (Winter, 1947), 154.

81. *Faulkner at Nagano*, p. 13.

82. *Who Owns America?*, p. 238.

83. *A Place on Earth*, p. 188.

4—A Troubled World—
"You'd Like Malindi"

1. *The Pocket History of the Second World War* (New York, *ca.* 1945), p. 16.

2. *For Whom the Bell Tolls* (New York, 1940). All page references are to the Scribner Library Edition.

3. *Cosmopolitan*, CVII (October, 1939), 104.

4. *Ibid.*    5. *Ibid.*, p. 102.

6. "The Friend of Spain: A Spanish Letter," *Esquire*, I (January, 1934), 26.

7. "A Paris Letter," *Esquire*, I (February, 1934), 156.

8. "Notes on the Next War," *Esquire*, IV (September, 1935), 19.

9. Selig Adler, *The Isolationist Impulse: Its Twentieth-Century Reaction* (New York, *ca.* 1957), p. 270.

10. (New York, 1926), pp. xi–xii.

11. *Ibid.*, pp. xii–xiii.

12. (New York, 1964), p. 76.

13. *The Fifth Column and The First Forty-Nine Stories* (New York, 1938), p. 308.

14. *Ibid.*, p. 323.    15. *Ibid.*, p. 329.

16. *To Have and Have Not* (New York, 1937). All page references are to this original edition.

17. *The Spanish Earth* (Cleveland, 1938), p. 10.

18. *Ibid.*, p. 19.    19. *Ibid.*, p. 34.

20. "The Writer and War," *The Writer in a Changing World*, ed. Henry Hart (New York, 1937), p. 69.

21. *Ibid.*, p. 70.    22. *Ibid.*, pp. 72–73.

23. *The Fifth Column and The First Forty-Nine Stories* (New York, 1938), p. 79. The Modern Library edition, *The Short Stories of Earnest Hemingway*, subtitled *The First Forty-Nine Stories and the Play "The Fifth Column,"* was published in 1942. Subsequently, a volume of the short stories only was published by Scribner's (1953).

24. *Ibid.*, p. vi.    25. *Ibid.*, pp. 97–98.

26. *Ibid.*, p. 42.    27. *Ibid.*, p. vi.

28. *Esquire*, X (December, 1938), 188.

29. *The Wound in the Heart* (Glencoe, Illinois; 1962), p. 175. This book contains an extensive "selected bibliography" of American writings and artistic creations inspired by the Spanish Civil War (pp. 235–77). It also classifies American responses according to the political orientations of the writers.

30. Bessie's review is reprinted in *Ernest Hemingway: Critiques of Four Major Novels*, ed. Carlos Baker (New York, 1962), pp. 90–94, from *New Masses*, XXXVII (November 5, 1940), 25–29.

31. *The Isolationist Illusion and World Peace* (New York, 1941), p. 9.

32. *Hemingway: The Writer as Artist*, 3rd ed. (Princeton, 1963), p. 228.

33. Carlos Baker, who calls the novel "a synecdochist's triumph," (*Ibid.*, p. 248.) considers it a modern epic comparable with the Homeric poems. The parallel will not stand up, however, because Homer wrote in an age when small, intimate bands of warriors were the major forces in international conflicts. The guerilla band in *For Whom the Bell Tolls* remains on the periphery of the struggle so that Hemingway can avoid treating the problems of impersonality in the high command of a modern fighting force.

34. Although Pablo's deterioration has a grave influence on the course of events in the novel, it is explained only by the early statement that the horses he stole from the Fascists "made him rich and as soon as he was rich he wanted to enjoy life" (p. 16). Hemingway implies what he may have been reluctant to express openly: that Pablo's biggest trouble is that, like some denizens of the Hotel Florida in *The Fifth Column*, he has become bored with a war that has lasted too long and the continual sacrifices it entails.

35. *The Writer in a Changing World*, p. 69.

36. *A Moveable Feast*, pp. 76–77.

37. Hemingway has Robert Jordan broach this very idea in *For Whom the Bell Tolls*, when, after Pilar tells him of the horrors of the execution of the fascists in the small town, Jordan observes, "If that woman could only write. He would try to write it and if he had luck and could remember it perhaps he could get it down as she told it" (p. 134).

### 5 – Salvation Squads:
### Commissar and Cross

1. *New York Times*, May 15, 1947, p. 30.

2. *Ibid.*, October 21, 1947, p. 1.

3. "Stepchild of the Muses," *North American Review*, CCXXXVI (December, 1933), 561.

4. *Eclipse* (London, 1935), p. 354.

5. *Ibid.*, pp. 92–95.    6. *Ibid.*, p. 120.

7. "Darling Bill— —," *Saturday Evening Post*, CCVII (April 20, 1935), 8–9, 94–105; "Five C's for Fever the Five," *Saturday Evening Post*, CCVIII (November 30, 1935), 10–11, 36–38.

8. *Washington Jitters* (New York, 1936), p. 182.

9. *Ibid.*, p. 272.

10. *Ibid.*, p. 287 (ellipsis in original).

11. *Johnny Got His Gun* (New York, 1939), pp. 298–99.

12. *Ibid.*, pp. 306–7.    13. *Ibid.*, pp. 308–9.

14. *Ibid.*, pp. 305–6. Joe "had a vision of himself as a new kind of Christ as a man who carries within himself all the seeds of a new order of things."

15. *John Steinbeck* (New York, 1961), p. 68.

16. Fletcher Pratt, "The Atlantic Bookshelf," *Atlantic Monthly*, January, 1940, unpaged.

17. John Cogley, *Report on Blacklisting, I: Movies* (n.p., 1956), p. 225.

18. *New York Times,* September 13, 1940, p. 27.

19. The twists in the Communist party line during the depression and World War II are outlined by Dorothy B. Jones in "Communism and the Movies," which is incorporated into John Cogley, *Report on Blacklisting, I: Movies,* pp. 196–304. Miss Jones, who was chief of the film reviewing and analysis section of the Office of War Information, points out that in the period between August, 1939, and June, 1941, Communists "denounced the war as an 'Imperialist' struggle—charging England and France with responsibility" and in the United States opposed the draft and the lend-lease program (p. 303).

20. *Saturday Review of Literature,* XXIII (February 15, 1941), 10.

21. *New York Times Book Review,* February 2, 1941, p. 6.

22. *Times Literary Supplement,* October 18, 1941, p. 517.

23. *Johnny Got His Gun,* p. 35.

24. (New York, *ca.* 1941), p. 300–1.

25. *Theatre Arts Monthly,* January, 1950, p. 87. The play (which is printed in full in this magazine, pp. 59–88) had apparently originally been designed as a propaganda barrage, for the author (who was out on bail pending the result of his appeal from his conviction for contempt of Congress) reports that when the play was trying out in Philadelphia, it mixed comedy with a serious message, but "the road audiences, however, howled at the comedy and displayed such an ominous hostility to the serious portions that we cut the latter entirely" (*Ibid.,* p. 58). The play lasted only thirteen performances in New York; Trumbo expressed a hope to do another play the following year, but he has never again been represented on Broadway—at least under his own name.

26. *New Yorker,* XVII (February 14, 1942), 59.

27. Harry Warfel, *American Novelists of Today* (New York, 1951), p. 187.

28. *Money and Man: A Survey of Monetary Experience* (New York, 1961), p. vii. This is a rewriting of *Money: The Human Conflict.*

29. *The Persian Journey of the Reverend Ashley Wishard and His Servant Fathi* (New York, 1937), p. 28.

30. *Ibid.*, p. 199.    31. *Ibid.*, p. 61.

32. *Ibid.*, p. 229.

33. *New York Herald-Tribune Books*, September 10, 1939, p. 1.

34. *Ararat* (New York, 1939), p. 388. All subsequent page references incorporated into the text are to this original edition.

35. *New Yorker*, XV (September 2, 1939), 54.

36. The viewpoint expressed through his novels infuses, however, even his technical writings about money, in which he argues constantly for the fiscal responsibility of government officials. He describes the sanctity of the coinage as "the idea that it is the duty of the state to avoid tampering with the money mechanism for personal or political objects, and that the duty of commercialists is to use money with restraint, as a means and not as an end" (*Money and Man*, p. 54). For its execution, this idea would require a firmer combination of virtue and good will than has usually been found.

37. Elgin Groseclose, *Introduction to Iran* (New York, 1947), pp. 181–82.

### 6 – Inquest and After:
### Phoenix as Laureate

1. "The Philosophical Joads," *College English*, II (January, 1941), 315–25.

2. "Jeffersonian Agrarianism in *The Grapes of Wrath*," *The University of Kansas City Review*, XIV (Winter, 1947), 154.

3. *The Wound in the Heart* (Glencoe, Illinois; 1962), pp. 192–93.

4. *The Winter of Our Discontent* (New York, 1961), p. 311.

### 7 – Epilogue: Beginners' Luck

1. The proletarian movement, which had been responsible for many first novels with social themes in the mid-thirties, had lost its impetus by 1939. Walter Rideout in *The Radical Novel in the United States 1900–1954* (Cambridge, Mass.; 1956) lists only six novels published during

the two years this study concentrates on, including Trumbo's *Johnny Got His Gun,* Wright's *Native Son,* and Albert Maltz's *The Underground Stream* (p. 298). The "lost generation" still found a few recruits. One of the most curious novels in the Hemingway manner at the end of the thirties is *Let Me Breathe Thunder* (New York, 1939), by William Attaway, a young Negro, who writes about a pair of white hoboes who pick up a young Mexican boy during their travels. The novel deals, like many of Hemingway's stories and much of Scott Fitzgerald's work, with the brutal and painful destruction of innocence by self-seeking and irresponsible people; but the artificially constructed tale sheds no light on conditions during the thirties or at any other time.

2. Stanley Edgar Hyman, "Some Trends in the Novel," *College English,* XX (October, 1958), 5–6, has noted what he calls the "pre-existentialist" characteristics of *Native Son,* but not its striking parallels with Camus's novels. Hyman's unwieldy label seems to me to obscure the fact that Wright was not so much converted to a new way of thinking by the existentialists he met in Paris as that he found the ideas of this group congenial to those that he had already independently developed.

3. "The Ordeal of Richard Wright," *College English,* XV (November, 1953), 92.

4. Translated by Stuart Gilbert (New York, 1948), p. 116.

5. *The Stranger,* trans. Stuart Gilbert, (New York: Vintage Books, 1959). All page references incorporated into the text are to this Vintage Books reprint.

6. *Saturday Review of Literature,* June 1, 1940, p. 4. Wright comments on the universality of his story when he remarks: "I made the discovery that Bigger Thomas was not black all the time; he was white, too, and there were literally millions of him, everywhere" (p. 17). The text of this article was also published separately as a promotional brochure.

7. *Native Son* (New York, 1940). All page references incorporated into the text are to this original edition.

8. *The Confidence-Man: His Masquerade* (New York: Grove Press, 1949), pp. 172–73.

9. *Ebony,* January, 1951, p. 84.

10. *New York Times Book Review*, August 20, 1939. The text of the full-page advertisement was reproduced from the *Book-of-the-Month Club News*.

11. *Coronet*, September, 1958, p. 5.

12. *American Novelists of Today* (New York, 1951), p. 442.

13. These parallels are traced in J. Létargeez, "Robert Penn Warren's View of History," *Revue des langues vivantes*, XXII (November–December, 1956), 533–43. John Goodrum Miller's *Black Patch War* (Chapel Hill, N. C.; 1936) is an exciting reminiscence of one episode resulting from the struggle by one of the participants, but it does not provide a comprehensive history of the conflict. The best account by a contemporary reporter is Martha McCulloch-Williams' "The Tobacco War in Kentucky," *Review of Reviews*, XXXVII (February, 1908), 168–70.

14. *Night Rider* (New York, 1939). All page references in the text are to this original edition.

15. *All the King's Men* (New York, 1946), p. 462.

# INDEX